THE LAYOFF JOURNEY

FROM DISMISSAL TO DISCOVERY

THE LAYOFF JOURNEY

FROM DISMISSAL TO DISCOVERY

Navigating
the Stages of Grief
After Job Loss

Steve Jaffe

FIRST EDITION

Cover design by Patricia Folgar

ISBN 979-8-9923756-0-2 (Paperback)

ISBN 979-8-9923756-1-9 (eBook)

Library of Congress Control Number: 2025900654

Jaffe Marketing & Publishing
TheSteveJaffe.com

For my wife, Amoreena,
who has stood by me through every job loss.
Your love and strength have helped me transform my
setbacks into opportunities.

"One day, you will tell your story of how you
overcame what you went through,
and it will become someone else's survival guide."
- Brené Brown

Table of Contents

Preface

March 2001 was the first time I was laid off, and June 2023 was the most recent; I was laid off four times over those 22 years. Does this make me an expert on the subject? Suffice it to say I've spent the requisite 10,000 hours recovering from the effects of being involuntarily "let go." After the first time I was laid off in 2001, it took me years to fully process the stages of grief; in 2023, it only took a few months. I aim to use the lessons I've learned to help others process their job loss in months rather than years. I want to share my journey through multiple layoffs as an expert who understands the pain and grief that comes with it.

This is not a lofty self-help book penned by an Ivy League Ph.D. with a wealth of academic training. This book was born from real-life experiences, written by someone who's weathered the storm of job loss not once but four times. I'm not here to offer abstract theories; I'm here to share genuine, relatable experiences in an authentic tone. Consider this book your survival guide, a master class in navigating the grief of job loss, designed to help you successfully move past it.

Introduction

It's easy to let our jobs define our existence—and just as easy to let an involuntary separation define our identity. Shame, embarrassment, and self-doubt often accompany a layoff. However, the commonality of layoffs has been steadily increasing to the point where, in some sectors (like technology, finance, marketing, and media), it's not a question of if but when they will occur. For perspective, according to McMaster University sociology professor Art Budros, in 1979, fewer than five percent of Fortune 100 companies announced layoffs, but in 1994, almost 45% did. A McKinsey survey of 2,000 U.S. companies found that from 2008-2011 (during the recession and its aftermath), 65% resorted to layoffs. In 2022 alone, 17.6 million Americans were laid off, and it's estimated that 40% of Americans have experienced at least one layoff in their careers. These numbers aren't just statistics—they represent a vast community of individuals who have gone through the same destabilizing event, just like you and me.

In today's business climate of uncertainty, competition, and technological advances, employee reductions have become so commonplace that attaching a stigma to the experience seems silly. Simply put, layoffs are not a reflection of your abilities; rather, they are a byproduct of companies' singular focus on the bottom line. And the bottom line is this: layoffs are a quicker way to recoup revenue than increasing sales.

Regardless, here you are. Your job, paycheck, and source of pride have all been taken away. This is one of life's most challenging things to process—Mount Rushmore-level grief, on par with a divorce or the death of a loved one. It may take weeks, months, or even years until you can fully accept what's happened. In many ways, the time following a layoff reminds me of Scott Belsky's book *The Messy Middle: Finding Your Way Through the Hardest and Most Crucial Part of Any Bold Venture*. You're navigating an uncertain, challenging space between what was known and secure and what is yet to come; you're caught in limbo between the identity you once held as an employee and the unclear path toward your next role. You're literally—and figuratively—in the messy middle.

From my experience processing multiple layoffs, I've found that the emotional journey from dismissal to discovery follows a pattern aligned with the *Stages of Grief* created by Elizabeth Kübler-Ross. The original five stages were based on her observations working with terminally ill patients, but two additional stages were later added, resulting in the current seven. While there are various interpretations of the seven—and none are universal for processing all forms of grief, especially those tied to a layoff— they typically include Denial, Pain, Negotiation, Depression, Acceptance, Reconstruction, and Renewal. These stages of grief are not always linear, and it's common to experience several within the same day, or on some glorious days, none at all. Some stages may take longer to process than others, and some may never manifest. There isn't a single stage that's harder to navigate than the others; each of our circumstances and the grief we carry are unique to us.

This book aims to help you navigate this experience, or at the very least, see it for what it is: a temporary setback, not a life-altering judgment on your abilities, character, or capacity for future employment. You won't find resume-writing tips or job-interview best practices here. Instead, you'll find an empathetic sherpa ready to guide you through the stages of grief so that, when you land your next job, you're prepared for success.

The chapters ahead explore the seven stages as they pertain to a layoff. You'll find insights, real stories, facts, myths, and advice—all designed to help you navigate and validate this season of life. At the end of each chapter, you'll find exercises intended to cultivate intentionality and resilience while you heal and process your grief. My goal is to equip you with a strong foundation of coping skills, because without them, taking control of the situation and embarking on a job search can be especially challenging. By allowing yourself time to reflect, set boundaries, and create goals, you'll build the guardrails necessary to navigate the road ahead.

This experience will undoubtedly echo for years to come. But I hope, like me, you'll come to see the echo as a friendly reminder of the challenges you've overcome and a milestone of personal growth—not as a debilitating cacophony of negative noise.

To heal from any loss, you have to go through it. Thank you for allowing me to share the skills I've developed for navigating job loss successfully.

Now, let's get started.

Stage One: Denial

So you've been let go, laid off, made redundant, whacked, shit-canned, eliminated, involuntarily separated, or reassigned to the industry bench. Regardless of the name it was given, when faced with the reality of the situation, a wave of emotions will come crashing down, and disbelief will likely lead the charge. No matter how or when you move through the stages of grief, I can say with near certainty that the first thing you'll feel is the shock of realizing you have no control over the unfolding situation. You are not a willing participant; nothing you can say or do will prevent the inevitable. A "no-fault" termination has powerlessness baked into its definition. You're being let go because of business or economic conditions beyond your control. No amount of negotiation or reasoning will alter its course.

About 75% of US employees are "at-will," which means we can be terminated at any time for any reason (absent labor discrimination laws). Janice in Human Resources may give you a reason, but she's not required to do so. Perhaps the company over-shot their staffing needs, revenue is down, they lost a client, or there's a looming recession or global pandemic. Maybe a new executive wants to institute a company-wide or departmental reorganization. Maybe there's been a merger, and some positions have been made redundant.

Janice may tell you this, or she may not. Maybe you didn't even meet with Janice; perhaps you received an email that began with, "We regret to inform you…" In some instances, it may feel better knowing the reason. It could also just throw gasoline on the fire, since most reasons for layoffs are related to decisions made by the Executive Leadership Team, for which you're now paying the price.

I worked at a renowned advertising agency in San Francisco when I got married in January 2001. I was responsible for planning and buying all the media for the most prestigious account at the agency. Agencies measure prestige in two ways: how far the client would permit the agency to push the envelope in terms of creativity (which leads to awards, aka the Holy Grail), and by the size of their budget. This client would allow us to create innovative ads and was by far the largest source of revenue for the agency. That was during the first dot-com explosion when agencies in San Francisco were awash in tech clients. Most of those clients weren't focused on building a solid business model or loyal customer base; they were focused on appealing to Wall Street for the fast cash infusion of an IPO. However, we considered ourselves lucky because our client had all the cash they needed to fund their business goals, our desire for awards and big media spending.

Their parent company was WorldCom. In case you're not familiar with WorldCom, they were a telecommunications company that committed accounting fraud (overstated assets by more than $11 billion) and underwent one of the largest bankruptcies in U.S. history. Thanks to the 2005 documentary

Enron: The Smartest Guys in the Room, more folks remember the Enron accounting scandal from the same period than WorldCom. Regardless, Enron, WorldCom, Tyco, and others started the first dot-com implosion in the early spring of 2001.

One March morning, fresh from a wedding and honeymoon and generally feeling optimistic about the future, I was meeting with a media vendor to discuss buying outdoor ads in various markets to support our award-winning campaign. This meeting was held in a room where a one-way mirror looked into an adjacent conference room. The small room and corresponding mirror were designed to support focus groups in the conference room. Focus groups are how agencies test creative concepts to learn which ideas resonate with the intended audience; the mirror allows observers to monitor feedback without disturbing the focus group. As I was meeting with the vendor, I could see some members of the Leadership Team and Human Resources in the adjacent conference room through the one-way mirror. They sat on one side of the big conference table, while various team members were escorted in and offered a seat directly across from them. I was focused on my meeting and couldn't hear what was being said through the wall, but judging by everyone's faces, it seemed serious. The meetings were short, and some paperwork from HR was passed on to my colleagues.

Our Office Manager entered the room where I was and asked me to come to the conference room. I asked her if it could wait until my meeting with the vendor was finished, but she politely yet firmly said no. I apologized to the vendor, told her I'd be right back, and excused myself. The vendor could see everything in the conference room through the one-way mirror.

As I entered the conference room, it was as solemn as a funeral. Sad and concerned faces. Brief sentences, long pauses.

The client was cutting their budget, the agency was cutting staff. Today was my last day. COBRA. Severance. Please clean out your desk. Immediately. Thank you for your service.

Getting laid off is an anxiety-producing event. Full stop. My body's immediate reaction was, well, shock. How could this happen? Why me? Surely, there must be some mistake! Soon to follow was shortness of breath, elevated heart rate, and a dry mouth. I felt numb, as if a strange haze took over my entire being. It was the opposite of feeling present and grounded. Suddenly, my future had become a giant black hole absorbing and casting doubt on everything in it. And I hadn't even left the conference room yet.

Minutes before, I was focused on the future by planning our client's next successful media campaign. At another time, I may have been writing an email, typing a Slack message, planning the day's tasks, or working through my to-do list. Regardless, all those projects were now essentially complete. But not because I completed them. Someone else would be doing that. The ownership, pride, and maybe even joy I felt for these projects were taken instantly. There wouldn't be an opportunity to hit send on that email, return that Slack message, or complete the meeting. My lunch appointment with co-workers would go on without me (with my layoff likely being the primary topic of conversation). In only a few minutes, my world had turned on its axis.

Similar types of layoffs would unfold across San Francisco in similar conference rooms throughout the spring. A few weeks after receiving my marching orders, my new bride was in one of those conference rooms, sitting opposite her leadership team and the ever-present, interchangeable, and ubiquitous Janice from Human Resources. There we were, newlyweds in the literal and figurative spring of our lives, collecting unemployment—our hopes and dreams crushed under the weight of a bursting dot-com bubble.

That was the first time I was let go from a job due to circumstances beyond my control. I didn't know then that a career in advertising and marketing would ensure this wouldn't be my last. It took me years to process this experience. It was hard to correlate what should have been one of the happiest times of my life (being young and newly married) with a feeling like the rug was pulled out from under me (and my wife). I was rewarded with an unemployment check in return for my success on this prestigious account. I mistakenly thought hard work and success would be rewarded with job security. That experience would expose that myth and many others. To make matters worse, the dot-com implosion in the spring of 2001 was closely followed by September 11, 2001. Things went from bad to worse. The economy and the country were in tatters; that was not an ideal time to be unemployed and looking for a job.

The unknown (at the time) downside of being young and mildly successful is that never having faced true adversity meant I had zero coping skills. I didn't know the importance of a support network. I had no idea (nor did I care) about the benefits of a healthy lifestyle for managing a crisis. Life had not prepared me for budgeting against the financial impact of an unemployed two-person household. Most importantly, I didn't understand the power of negative thoughts and my propensity for depression and anxiety. To say life caught me unprepared would be a dramatic understatement.

The Grace of Denial

The shockwave of the initial minutes, hours, and days after a layoff has likely left you with an accompanying daze. This is the gift known as denial. Elisabeth Kuber-Ross, the Swiss-American psychiatrist who pioneered the stages of grief, famously said, "Denial helps us to face our feelings of grief…it's nature's way of letting in only as much as we can handle." It's not so much that life only gives us what we can handle; rather, our bodies limit how much we can process at any given time. Denial is a healthy psychological defense mechanism for overwhelming and stressful situations.

Sometimes, our world moves quicker than our minds can process; denial allows our brains time to catch up. It's a natural and common reaction to facing the sudden and unexpected existential question of "Who am I without this job?" The brain's primary function is to ensure survival, and in this instance, your brain registers the situation and this question as a threat to survival. Think of denial as a life preserver that's keeping you from drowning in pain. Denial provides the calm before the storm.

Denial may manifest as emotional detachment or avoidance of the subject altogether. You may experience a memory gap regarding the details surrounding your layoff. Physical symptoms such as headaches, irritability, or general fatigue may present themselves. The body tends to release its grip on denial once the chaos of the moment and the initial fears and anxiety subside. Denial keeps us safe, and only after we feel safe can we experience all the emotions of the moment. Experiencing denial after you've been laid off is normal and natural; it's our body's innate way of coping with some situations, but unchecked, it can become a lasting barrier to embracing the reality of the situation.

The Myth of Meritocracy

As you search for answers and settle into the reality of the situation, you'll find that layoffs are often indiscriminate—and sometimes even discriminatory. Some of the smartest, hardest-working, and most talented people may get laid off, while some of the most ineffective, unproductive, and disengaged employees remain.

I had a coworker who requested a day off six months in advance so she could travel to attend a big concert for the weekend. She regularly worked weekends, so giving the six-month notice seemed an excellent way to ensure she'd finally have a much-needed and well-deserved break. However, days before the approved time off, her boss politely asked if she could forgo the PTO and work over the weekend. Of course, saying no wasn't an acceptable answer, so she worked that weekend just like most others and missed the opportunity to see her favorite performer. A few months later, she was laid off regardless. With seemingly little regard, the company let one of its most hard-working, responsible, and considerate employees go.

Michael Young, often called the most significant sociologist of the past century, coined meritocracy over 60 years ago. His equation was, "IQ + effort = merit." Today, meritocracy is the first and perhaps biggest myth of the modern workplace. Rewritten for today's corporate world, his equation would likely calculate any combination of Personal Relationship + Likability + Conformity = Favorability (aka job security). That favorability will often eclipse work quality, performance, and output. We've all witnessed family and close friends of the leadership team retain their jobs while the organization faced a reduction in force. We've all had a coworker who was not particularly "high-performing" maintain their job security or even receive a promotion due to their "favorability" within the organization, rather than their IQ or effort.

I once worked at an advertising agency that hired the client's son. He was a lot of fun and excelled at the "play hard" part of "work hard, play hard." He often played hard on a work night and would come in tired from the prior night's frivolity. On those occasions, he would fall asleep at his desk located outside the office of a Senior Vice President in the agency. He would have been swiftly but politely escorted out if he were anyone but a client's son. However, the only way the agency could let him go was when they lost the account of which his father was the President.

When I was laid off from the ad agency, I was an intelligent, high performer. I worked long hours and put my heart and soul into the job. One of the best compliments I ever received was from the WorldCom client, who told me that I gave her peace of mind because she knew I was always thinking about her business. Unfortunately, IQ + effort did not equate to job security.

While strict hiring laws are in place to minimize discrimination, they are difficult to measure and enforce for layoffs (or if a company wants to hire a client's son). That means there are limited regulatory requirements related to the impact of layoffs on the workplace composition of race, gender, or age. The point is that layoffs are non-linear, inequitable, subjective, unpredictable, and always outside of our control.

When Bad Gets Worse

There is no good way to get laid off. I've been laid off in person by caring and compassionate people, and I've been laid off over Zoom by folks who didn't seem to care very much. I've heard of people getting laid off via email. Employees have been laid off on vacation or family and medical leave. Women have been laid off mid-pregnancy or even while in labor. Sales reps have had their credit cards shut off mid-business trip without notice. Sometimes, they just shut the computer off. Or deactivate your key card. People have been laid off just days before the Christmas holidays or even *during* the holidays. Often, folks will learn about pending layoffs via an announcement during a company all-hands meeting. However, it's not uncommon to learn the news from watching or reading the news, as companies often share information with Wall Street before their employees. Sometimes, rumors begin and go unaddressed by leadership, which is a tacit acknowledgment, thereby removing the need for any difficult announcement. Companies talk a lot about culture, and the way they communicate layoffs is a good indicator of it.

The most recent horrific layoff stories I've heard come from the social media platform formerly known as Twitter. Since Elon Musk took over the company in October 2022, approximately 6,000 employees have been laid off, with many being let go merely a week after his arrival. As a result, Musk has faced multiple class-action lawsuits, including those accusing the company of discrimination and failure to pay severance. Some were notified via an email to their personal accounts, with the subject line ominously reading, "Your Role at Twitter." The body of the email contained a simple declaration: "Today is your last day working at the company." Many received this email at midnight and did not check their personal email before arriving at work that day. Therefore, they came to find that their badges had been deactivated, and they couldn't enter the building, only to be turned away at the door. One employee who was already in the building found they were trapped in the parking garage because their pass no longer worked. Similar scenarios were repeated at another Musk company, Tesla, when he laid off 14,000 employees in 2024.

Musk often insinuates that if you work hard enough and are smart enough, you'll survive and thrive at his companies (IQ + effort = merit). However, a few painful examples tell a different story. Esther Crawford, a Chief Executive of Payments at Twitter, famously tweeted a picture of herself sleeping on the floor of her office with a caption that read: "When your team is pushing round the clock to make deadlines, sometimes you #SleepWhereYouWork." She was subsequently laid off. Then there is the story of Nico Murillo, a Tesla Production Supervisor for five years who often slept in his car (to avoid a lengthy commute), showered at the office, and microwaved dinner in the breakroom. One morning at 4:30 a.m., when he logged into his computer, he learned his account had been deactivated. He then received an email (to his personal account) that read, in short, "Your position has been eliminated." Those, along with many other former Twitter and Tesla employees, and thousands of other employees at hundreds of different companies, displayed similar dedication to their employers, only to be reciprocated by learning they were victims of a "simplified operating model."

How To: Process Emotions in Healthy Ways

In the coming weeks, a lot of feelings are going to surface. Whatever they are, take the time to acknowledge and accept them without judgment. Recognize that all of these emotions are valid and understandable given the circumstances. Give yourself the freedom to experience those emotions fully without trying to suppress or deny them; it's important to create space.

I recommend starting and ending the day by checking in with yourself to identify how you're feeling. You may call this meditating or even praying. It doesn't matter what you call it, how you do it, or when. It only matters that you find a way to listen and validate your experience. I've found the practice called mindful meditation to be very beneficial. But don't get scared by the hippy-dippy name. It's just a way of taking deep breaths and focusing on how your body feels in the moment. It's actually very simple and effective in stressful situations.

Sit comfortably and close your eyes.
Breathe in for four seconds and out for four seconds.
While you're doing this, notice how your body feels.
Start with your toes and work your way up to your head.
Notice any sensations and tensions in your body.
As you breathe and connect to your body, accept any feelings.
Observe what you feel without judging whether anything is right or wrong or feeling the need to correct it.

Mindful meditation can be done in 30 seconds or as long as you'd like. It can be helpful when faced with anxiety-producing events or any traumatic experience. It can be done in your car after you've received the news of your layoff or at home after they've turned off your computer. It's a great way to bring peace and stillness into a chaotic situation. This way of pressing pause and checking in with yourself will be a great exercise to learn and have in your toolbox as you develop the coping skills necessary to move through this experience.

However you choose to connect to your emotions, remember that this is about being gentle with yourself—practicing self-compassion by treating yourself with kindness and understanding. Validate your feelings by offering yourself the same empathy and support you would provide a friend experiencing a similar situation. Remind yourself that it's okay to feel like you do, and you deserve compassion and care. Something has been taken from you. Perhaps something that defined your identity. Maybe something that gave you immense pride and joy. At a minimum, it provided financial support for yourself and possibly your loved ones. It's normal to feel broken by this experience.

Once you've listened to and identified the emotions, it's essential to express them. Journaling is a purposeful and healthy way, as is talking to a friend, mentor, family member, former coworker, or therapist. The support group you create in this early period will become an important new community to replace the one you've lost. Creative outlets such as music, art, cooking, or dance are also great forms of expression. Expressing these emotions will allow you to release tension and gain clarity around your feelings. This becomes the avenue by which you find community, validation, and acceptance.

Roadmap Exercise: Finances

Most often, the immediate concern for the newly unemployed is money. If you're lucky, you saved for a rainy day. Congratulations! It's pouring rain. Now is the time to determine how much cash you have in reserve, what you may be able to cut, and what sources of income you may be able to access to float your period of unemployment.

Confronting the reality of your financial situation will be difficult (especially considering it can be difficult even when you have a steady paycheck coming in). But getting a clear and early picture of your finances will be essential to understanding how to maneuver this season of uncertainty.

1. Gather all documents and statements in order to see where you sit financially. What reserves do you have in the bank? Did you get severance and/or are you eligible for unemployment benefits?
2. Make a list of your monthly expenses. Account for the big stuff (obviously) like mortgage or rent and car payments, but don't forget about the small stuff like recurring subscriptions (Netflix, phone apps, etc). They're sneaky and they add up.
3. Take it one month at a time. For the next 30 days, determine how much money will go in (income) and out (expenses). After addressing the first month, move on to the next. It's common for the job hunt to last six months or longer, so it would be smart to account for at least that period of time.
4. By looking at it from an elevated view, you can easily see if (and especially when) cuts need to be made. Consider which costs aren't absolutely necessary and deduct them accordingly, adding those amounts to your monthly income.

Helpful tip: When assessing your finances, be sure to factor in your broader healthcare needs. During your brief conversation with Janice, she probably mentioned continuing health coverage and COBRA. You'll want to carefully weigh all the options to determine which path best fits you. If ongoing healthcare through the company isn't on the table, that's helpful to know as you project the upcoming months.

Reframe: A Lucky Escape

Our minds have a way of believing what we tell them. If you're trapped inside a victim mentality, flip the script and think about it as life handing you a reset button. Maybe you didn't love your job, or your industry is shrinking. Maybe you liked your job, but your gut said it wasn't the right path for you. Either way, this is your "get out of jail" free card.

Stage Two: Pain

If denial provides temporary shelter before the coming storm, this stage represents the inevitable arrival of the hurricane of pain. Once the daze of the event has passed, the situation becomes painfully real. There are so many emotions: shame, embarrassment, humiliation, loss, and worthlessness—just to name a few. However, anger, one of the most basic human emotions, is likely to manifest as a byproduct of those feelings.

I've often felt an overwhelming anger over the circumstances of my layoffs. The injustice of it all! The personal sacrifices you made for the job suddenly seem pointless. The crappy salary, long nights, and forfeited weekends feel wasted. Maybe those long nights and weekends were voluntary, or perhaps they were the result of pressure to prioritize work over your well-being. Regardless, the loyalty you gave to your employer has not been reciprocated. All the company and team outings, with their forced camaraderie in the name of team building, now feel incredibly insincere. You may feel resentment toward your former boss and those in leadership. After all, your life is in turmoil, and not only are they responsible, but they've likely retained their jobs at your expense.

Frankly, who wouldn't be upset about the situation? Frustrated about the projects that will go uncompleted. Bitter about the sudden loss of work friends (and missing the recap of *Game of Thrones* in the break room). Angry about being locked out of your work computer and unable to access months or years of achievements. Embarrassed that you were escorted out of the office with your belongings in a box. All of these are 100% legitimate reactions!

The morning of my second layoff began just like any other: suited up and caffeinated amidst a snarled commute. I had a morning meeting with my boss, the Senior Vice President of Marketing and Communications, for which, despite traffic, I arrived early. I believe in always being on time; more specifically, I subscribe to Vince Lombardi's idea of time: "If you're not early, you're late." Naturally, I was eagerly waiting outside my boss's office a few minutes before our scheduled meeting time. His office door was open, and I could hear him speaking with a woman. I only caught the end of their conversation.

Woman: "How do you think he's going to handle this?"

Boss: "It's just part of doing business; it is very common and happens all the time. I'm sure he'll understand and be fine."

I didn't understand then that my position was being eliminated. However, once I was called into his office and saw the woman sitting across the desk was Janice, I started to put it together. My boss had recently come from another company and was hired by the new CEO with whom he used to work. He had been systematically letting everyone in the marketing department go, only to replace them with folks he and the new CEO had previously worked with.

I had been with the company for nearly five years by then, so I was one of the last on the list, but I was on the list nonetheless.

It was my turn, with an apparent expectation that I'd be "fine" because I understood the ways of the corporate world. Here's the only thing I understood: the business world was complete bullshit.

Was I angry? Absolutely. I wanted to tell him that his need to lay off all those great people so he could reunite a band composed of his former subordinates was absurd, that his ego was affecting so many people's lives in ways he couldn't even fathom. I wanted him to know that letting everyone go only to replace them with people he had existing relationships with was poor leadership and a literal cliché. How I didn't respect him for all the times he interrupted our meetings to take a call from his interior designer. How I found him pathetic. Those were some of the thoughts that ran through my mind as Janice explained my severance package.

But because he was my boss and because he thought I'd see the situation as a perfectly normal business-related occurrence, it created a strange power dynamic. It forced me to conform to his expectations. If I were to react angrily, I would lose his respect and undermine any opportunity for a positive reference in the future. To make matters worse, it was easy to think my emotions weren't valid because of that social conditioning. It was as if there was a secret handshake that, by keeping the peace, we were forced to either acknowledge or deny. If we don't accept those social mores and norms, and instead react with anger or frustration, we risk banishment from the white-collar world altogether.

So there I was, sweating underneath my suit, trying to remain calm while simultaneously going numb. I forced a smile, being painfully polite, while biting my tongue. Thank you for the opportunity. See you next time, Janice.

The Psychology of Pain

A chemical reaction occurs in all of us due to painful stimuli. Burn your arm on an iron? Botch a presentation? Get unfollowed on a dating site? Lose a job? The subsequent sensations of each—acute physical discomfort, failure, rejection, loss—all trigger the nervous system to send the same signal to the brain: Distress! Threat! Pain! Although the brain doesn't process emotional and physical pain identically, research on neural pathways suggests a substantial overlap between the two experiences. Therefore, our reactions appear to be similar.

Our blood pressure rises, and our breathing quickens or becomes shallow. Stress hormones release. Muscles tense. Endorphins flood our bodies. Maybe there's shaking, nausea, or sweating. Negative emotions run rampant. And then we're faced with everyone's favorite dilemma: how to respond to the stressful, delicate, and high-pressure situation when we seemingly have no control over our minds or bodies.

The most common type of stress response, or at least the one people tend to know, is the "fight-or-flight" response. It evolved as a survival mechanism that allowed our caveman and cavewoman ancestors to react quickly to life-threatening situations. Come face to face with a saber-toothed tiger? Our body's cascade of stress hormones produces well-orchestrated physiological changes that give us the energy to either fight the threat off or flee to safety.

Similar to the way additional stages of grief have been added to the original five that Elisabeth Kübler-Ross created, another response has been added to the fight-or-flight response: freeze. It involves an immediate stilling of movement, with vigilance to the threat, and in preparation for the active fight-or-flight response. If our brain were to trigger a freeze reaction when face to face with a hungry tiger, we'd quickly become lunch. But if Janice from HR calmly tells us that after "a careful evaluation of our business operations, market conditions, and future goals, we have made the difficult decision to implement a company-wide reduction in workforce," neither running out of the room nor punching her in the face are acceptable responses.

That is likely why, upon learning about a layoff, my body has most often reacted by freezing up. In a haze, my body is trying to process what's happening by triggering adrenaline, which causes hot flashes, sweating, dry mouth, and heart palpitations. Freezing in stressful situations is a modern solution to modern problems. While our amygdalas don't distinguish a difference between the saber-toothed tiger and Janice, social conditioning requires this third reaction. The chemical activity throughout our body is identical regardless of which circumstance we are faced with.

Irrespective of which survival mechanism your body immediately went into, a layoff's physical, emotional, and social impact can be profound and long-lasting. Layoffs have been linked to an increase in divorce, depression, and cardiovascular disease (just to name a few).

Even if a person is healthy, the odds of developing a new health condition rise by 83% in the first 15 to 18 months following a layoff. A study published in *Health Economics* attributed this to the chronic stress of unemployment, financial insecurity, and loss of health insurance. Another study from *The American Journal of Epidemiology* noted that prolonged unemployment leads to higher rates of lifestyle-related diseases such as obesity, diabetes, and alcohol-related disorders. If Mark Zuckerberg had known about these effects, would he have thought twice about laying off nearly 21,000 employees within two years?

I lived in Las Vegas for ten years, and I've often told people that Vegas could magnify any personal vice. If you begin your residence there with a slight problem with drinking, just wait. Perhaps food, gambling, shopping, sex, or drugs are your weaknesses upon arrival—just wait. Most people can barely handle a weekend in Vegas, so good luck spending ten years. But that's the subject of another book. Just like Las Vegas, a layoff will magnify whatever problem you already have. Rocky marriage, financial shortcomings, eating disorders, anxiety, alcoholism, depression? A layoff can exacerbate all of them.

That is why I'm a strong proponent of a whole-body approach to managing pain. As demonstrated by the statistics above, the trauma of a layoff and its associated effects can be severe. For example, my first layoff exacerbated my pre-existing propensity for depression and anxiety in a way that led to a prescription for Prozac. Mitigating the emotional and physical toll on your body is why I stress the importance of developing healthy coping skills during this time. The skills we use (or don't use) to manage the pain of this layoff will dictate the impact of this experience.

Left unchecked and unmanaged, things can quickly get out of control. Those drinks you had in the first few days after a layoff to numb the pain can easily turn into a nightly occasion. The comfort food you may have delivered to your apartment can become a daily source of comfort and eventually create discomfort in your clothes. Dealing with the effects of a layoff can be particularly challenging for someone with non-normative mental health. This situation will likely introduce many new stressors needing active and regular management. All that to say, our bodies naturally associate this experience with trauma. It's up to us to tell our bodies how we're going to process that trauma. When thoughts of shame or embarrassment creep in, remember that 40% of all Americans have been laid off at least once. It's alright to allow ourselves some indulgences during this period. Just don't let those indulgences become such a regular occasion that they become routine to a destructive point.

The Other Side of Layoffs

Work friends are a special kind of friend. They are your crew, your squad, and your tribe, the ones you share your foxhole with. They have your back when things get dicey. They are relationships contained within the confines of office walls, cubicles, Slack channels, or, more often, Zoom chats. The depth and investment of these friendships range from exchanging pleasantries to knowing what Brian from Accounting's daughter is wearing to prom. There are some special coworkers—you know the ones— who became your second family, with whom you spent more time than your first family. You shared inside jokes, liked the same places for lunch, and went to the same places together for drinks after work. You shared dreams, secrets, and grievances. You counted on their support, opinions, and presence. And then suddenly, they were gone.

More than likely, you didn't get to say goodbye to those friends. You couldn't tell them how much they meant to you. Couldn't give a farewell hug. Even if you were given the opportunity, you would likely have been in shock, anger, or denial and couldn't articulate the importance of their friendship. The sudden end to your workday meant a sudden end to these relationships. The people you usually would turn to during difficult times at work are now unavailable. Minutes ago, you were members of the same club and shared the same clubhouse. Now you're an outsider. Your pass has been revoked, literally and figuratively.

Cue another layer of emotional pain.

If a feeling of loss defines the entire layoff experience, losing these relationships is one of the most profound. There's so much left undone and unsaid. So much unraveling. Former athletes and military personnel often say the one thing they miss most is the camaraderie of their teammates. It's easy to forget about the projects and deliverables that will go unmet; it's not easy to forget about the special people you worked with. Mourning those folks will be as crucial as mourning the loss of tangible things like your paycheck and health benefits. There are many things I've forgotten about past jobs, but I still remember many of the special people I worked with. I have been fortunate that many of my work friendships have stood the test of time and circumstance. While many friendships survive the separation caused by a layoff, most won't.

One of the most significant factors is that remaining employees grapple with their own emotional turmoil in the immediate aftermath of a layoff. While they may feel relief from still having a job, this is often overshadowed by feelings of guilt, anger, and anxiety. Survivor guilt is a very real thing. Generally, it sets in when people survive traumatic events like combat, a natural disaster, or mass layoffs. Layoff survivors bear the psychological impact in significant and even long-lasting ways: heightened anxiety over job security, paranoia and distrust of management, and extreme burnout due to increased workloads. (Remember the project you were working on that was going to be finished by someone else? Guess who's the beneficiary of increased responsibilities due to your sudden and unexpected departure?) The bottom line is they're dealing with their own pain and grief.

Your former work community will go on without you, and you will need to go on without them. You may remain friends with a few of them, but the common bond you shared about the trials and tribulations of the job no longer exists. To remain friends, you need to find a new common ground. But sometimes, that only serves to prolong the feeling of separateness.

Exiting With Goodwill

During this stage, you may want to lash out. I'm not suggesting you want to slash your boss's tires (although maybe that thought crossed your mind), but you may feel a strong urge to gossip or disparage your former employer. You've likely heard the phrase, "Don't burn any bridges," and now is the time to take that to heart. The saying refers to a Roman military practice in which soldiers burned bridges to stop the enemy from advancing further or to stop enemies from escaping once they entered a territory. Once burned, there would be no way for them to retreat or move forward. It was a savage and final way to ensure the original path could not be restored.

Most industries are surprisingly small, and you may see these former colleagues again. Imagine how uncomfortable it would be if you bump into them at a trade show or conference and there's weird, awkward tension. Or what if Janice's cousin is the hiring manager at a new company? While your job may have ended, your network shouldn't suffer. That network is likely what's going to help you land on your feet.

Some companies actively assist employees in finding their next job. They may reach out across their social media or personal networks with references and connections. They may even know someone who's hiring for a position that matches your exact experience. It's been estimated that up to 70-80% of jobs never appear on job sites. This "hidden job market" is accessed via networking, recruiters, relationships, and referrals. From personal experience, 25% of my jobs were never publicized.

All that to say, leaving on friendly terms preserves access to goodwill and potential future opportunities. This is why it's imperative to leave with your reputation intact, regardless of how you feel. It's not about denying your pain; it's about choosing the right time and place to express it.

The temporary satisfaction of denigrating your former employer may feel good in the moment, but it can have serious consequences. Taking the high road in this situation can not only safeguard future professional opportunities but also preserve your peace of mind. Think about the last time you lost your cool. While it may have felt justified (and even satisfying) in the moment, chances are you replayed the situation endlessly—oh, the tossing and turning!—and wished you had responded differently. Let's not add more regret to our pile of pain. As the late Spanish writer and philosopher Baltasar Gracián said, "It is better to sleep on things beforehand than lie awake about them afterward."

Now is the time to demonstrate professionalism and decorum. The best advice I can offer is to assume that anything you say to a former co-worker will be shared with the CEO and the entire leadership team. Imagine your words will be repeated in the next "All Hands" meeting or across team chats. If you don't want it repeated, don't say it. Unless, of course, you're sharing feedback anonymously on Glassdoor—but even then, I recommend waiting at least 90 days after your layoff to post. This waiting period allows time for emotions to settle, providing you with a more balanced perspective for your review. As we've learned, layoffs are part of doing business. A terrible part that occurs far too often. But from the company's perspective, there's an unspoken agreement that they are a necessary—albeit unfortunate—response to economic cycles.

Keep this in mind if you stay in touch with co-workers who try to commiserate about your ex-boss, workplace, or leadership in an effort to connect or offer comfort. It's important to set boundaries with these friends. Establishing limits during these interactions will help create a sense of safety and control in your environment—exactly what's needed for the journey toward healing and recovery.

How To: Release Frustration

When physical pain is unrelieved, it triggers a stress response in the body. The same is true with emotional pain. As we discussed in the Denial phase, it's vital to have an outlet to process your emotions. But how you process the fiery ball of anger and frustration in your gut may call for something more than journaling or art class.

The most obvious action is to get your blood pumping with exercise. Aerobic exercise, in particular, has been shown to increase one's emotional resilience to acute stress; the natural release of norepinephrine, dopamine, and serotonin are among the best ways to combat anxiety, depression, and anger. The key here is to pick an activity where the continuous movement and effort won't allow time for the mind to dwell. Drift, maybe. Dwell, no. Think running, rowing, circuit training, or even jumping rope. Of course, if you need something more explosive (I get it), you can hit a punching bag or take up kickboxing. Whatever it is, make sure you sweat. Consider this a detox from your toxic former boss, co-workers, or company.

Not into working out? Consider going to a rage room or even just screaming it out somewhere that doesn't result in the police being called. The important thing is to *get it out* (doing so in a responsible and appropriately timed manner is equally important). Nothing good will come from keeping it inside.

As you move forward, you will face triggers of the work-life you lost. You might run into a former colleague, hear that the big project finally launched, or see a sale for the same coffee pot they had at the office. Once, the smell of popcorn triggered a complete breakdown for me, unearthing grief I hadn't fully processed. These moments are beyond your control, but do yourself a favor: avoid deliberately seeking out triggers. That might mean steering clear of the company website or resisting the urge to gossip about the IT guy with an ex-colleague. Don't poke the bear.

Roadmap Exercise: Guiding Principles

Poorly executed corporate mission statements are as ubiquitous as poorly executed layoffs: *To be the best in the industry and provide excellent customer service. Make the world a better place through innovation and excellence. To empower our customers to achieve their dreams.*

Originally, mission statements served a purpose and held meaning. Unfortunately, those days have largely passed. Many companies are now left with lofty, ambiguous, and often unachievable goals like the examples above. However, well-crafted mission statements still matter. Good companies treat them as a North Star—a guiding force that helps navigate challenges and maintain course during turbulent times.

Polaris, commonly known as the North Star, is the brightest star in the northern constellation of Ursa Minor. It remains nearly stationary as the northern sky revolves around it, making it an enduring tool for navigation. For centuries, sailors have used Polaris to find their way, no matter their location. Similarly, when a company experiences the inevitable push and pull of business, its North Star—a clear mission and set of principles—can keep it aligned and steady. In business, strong North Stars are the result of careful consideration and rigorous testing. They stem from a shared understanding of a company's purpose, values, and principles.

On a personal level, people often refer to their goals as their own North Star: *I will run a marathon this year (physical goal), save 10% from each paycheck for retirement (financial goal), and practice meditation or prayer once daily (spiritual goal).* These fixed visions provide direction, constancy, and motivation. But how does one identify the guiding principles that shape their vision?

Guiding principles are our foundational beliefs or philosophies that inform our choices and behavior. Examples include integrity, gratitude, or a growth mindset. They are deeply held personal values or tenets that remain constant regardless of our circumstances. For instance, if integrity is one of your guiding principles, honesty will underpin all your interactions. Such principles help manifest the best version of yourself while steering you away from negative traits. When these values become your North Star, they influence everything—your conduct, approach, thoughts, interactions, attitude, decisions, and performance.

What are your guiding principles?

_____

_____

_____

_____

_____

_____

If this is a new line of thought for you, here is a rudimentary offering: Start by identifying 3-5 personal ethics or ideals that resonate deeply, such as _honesty, resilience, patience,_ and _achievement._ Then, personalize each value by turning it into actionable statements. _Be honest in word and deed. Maintain a positive outlook. Practice patience. Compete to win._

Once you've written your guiding principles, take it a step further by reflecting on how each one could influence your decisions and actions over the next few months. Guiding principles should actively shape your behavior. For example, "Be honest in word and deed" during the first weeks after a layoff might mean avoiding gossip about your ex-employer and being transparent with loved ones about what you need—be it space, comfort, or support. By month two or three, it might mean ensuring your resume is truthful and being direct with prospective employers about your salary expectations. Your guiding principles remain constant, but how they manifest will evolve with time and circumstance.

Remember the strategic value of the North Star: It holds still while the entire sky moves around it.

Reframe: Refined Resilience

This is a great opportunity for self-reflection and self-discovery. Doing the "inside work" right now will allow you to chart a more mindful course full of firsthand knowledge and hard-won insights. Most importantly, it will empower you as you navigate current and future challenges and rebound from inevitable setbacks.

Stage Three: Negotiation

In the wee small hours following all four of my layoffs, I would often lie awake thinking I'd be offered my job back once they realized a mistake had been made. Because surely a mistake had been made. It's similar to how people cling to the hope of reconciliation after a breakup, not unlike King George's lament in *Hamilton*: "You'll be back." I believe this false hope of reconciliation is particularly exacerbated by the "no-fault" nature of many layoffs. When they tell you the decision is not a reflection of your performance but solely due to the circumstances within the company (*"It's not you, it's me"*), it can leave the door open to endless questions and wishful thinking.

What if I remind them of all my positive performance reviews or the KPIs (key performance indicators) I hit last quarter? What if I demonstrate my ROI to the company's bottom line? Should I offer to take a pay cut or transition into a different role? If only I had told them I just bought a new house and needed this job to pay the mortgage—surely they'd reconsider.

This stage of grief is all about negotiation—with yourself, possibly with your employer, maybe with the universe. It's often marked by a mental tug-of-war between reason and reality, filled with hypothetical scenarios starting with "what if" and "if only." At its core lies a deep, natural desire to maintain control over an uncontrollable situation.

Also likely: the compulsion to dissect all the various ways you could have been more efficient, the need to reevaluate your interactions with senior management, the inclination to regret the times you were late or called in sick, and the urge to scrutinize every perceived shortfall. The internal dialogue around what you could have done better and how the whole thing could have been avoided will be an itch you'll want to scratch like a dog licking a wound. But I implore you to resist allowing your inner Dr. Spock to examine this patient.

It's natural to reflect on past choices and wonder if things could have turned out differently. Three of my layoffs occurred because my position was eliminated. Two of those roles were experimental—positions that didn't exist at the organization before I arrived. After these layoffs, I went through multiple rounds of self-evaluation. I scrutinized the role, the expectations, the outcome, and what (if anything) I could have done differently.

There was no roadmap, template, or guidance around what worked or failed in the past. Starting from scratch, I built a solid proof of concept for each position and demonstrated clear ROI. But taking on these experimental roles was a considerable risk— one that ultimately didn't pay off. When the companies hit hard times, the patience to let the new role play out wore thin.

How could I have approached it differently? Were there other choices I could have made? Did I take too big of a risk?

In Kübler-Ross's original five stages of grief, this phase is referred to as bargaining. Negotiation and bargaining share a common thread: a desire to change, improve, or reach a resolution. In negotiation, this often means working toward a mutually beneficial agreement. In grief-related bargaining, the process is internal—seeking comfort or relief from pain. Both involve compromise, but the stakes are different. In negotiation, you might concede certain terms to reach an agreement. In bargaining through grief, the thoughts tend to sound like, *If I promise to do X, maybe Y will change.*

Since the loss in this case is your job—and you may still be grappling with severance terms while trying to regain control over a situation that feels deeply uncontrollable—this chapter will help you address both the practical and emotional aspects of this stage.

Where Logic Meets Emotions and Reality

The Age of Reason, also known as the Age of Enlightenment, was a period between the 17th and 18th centuries when rational thought helped propel civilization out of the Dark Ages. During this time, society began to emphasize rational evaluation of facts and data. Applied to a layoff situation, if one can understand their job loss without emotion, they may be able to accept it—at least theoretically. But what happens when the situation defies rational explanation? And what happens when removing emotion isn't an option?

When we face a layoff, we face a complex conflict between our reasoning, our feelings, and the stark reality of the situation. We suddenly have no job, but we feel strongly that we deserve to have one! There's a mountain of evidence supporting our past successes—early mornings, late nights, and epic sacrifices. We've proven ourselves to be dedicated, prompt, responsible, and hard-working. We have the receipts, too: the long weekends spent over-delivering, the creative solutions to problems that shouldn't have been ours to solve, and the loyalty we've shown. Our egos tell us this shouldn't be happening—that we've earned immunity through hard work and commitment. Yet our emotions pull us in another direction, stirring anger, sadness, and even guilt, making us question if we could have done more or been more.

It's not just the sense of unfairness; it's the inner turmoil. We logically understand that companies must make tough decisions, but emotionally, it feels deeply personal. The sudden loss of identity, security, and purpose hits like a tidal wave. The logic of restructuring cannot alleviate the emotional toll of being pushed aside after pouring so much of ourselves into our work. Our feelings of anger, betrayal, and confusion fight against the facts: no amount of individual effort could have shielded us from this.

In this way, a layoff is more than just a job loss; it's the collision of two opposing forces. On one side is our internal narrative, rooted in self-worth, emotional stakes, the tangible proof of our performance, and a belief in justice for hard work. On the other side is the often cold, impersonal reality of business decisions. Our reasoning, built on the undeniable evidence of our dedication, skills, and value, clashes violently with the actions and rationale of others.

Once, I was the first person in a round of layoffs that would result in a 20% decrease in headcount. I couldn't help but think there was some significance to the fact that I was first. After the initial phase of anger and denial, I realized someone had to be first on the list, just like someone had to be last. No benefit could come from weaving a web of negative thoughts around the significance of an insignificant detail. It's clear to see the natural disconnect when looking for a logical reason for an illogical situation. If only it were as easy to recognize the same disconnect from the emotional impact.

When we're at the intersection of logic and emotions, we often make inferences about our performance and the value we provided to the organization. Based on firsthand experience, those inferences are very dark paths that should be avoided. Nobody who understands the current state of business and the brutality of the corporate world would ever equate a person's worth with a layoff. Anyone who does pass judgment certainly has never been directly affected by one.

Meta Founder, Chairman, and CEO Mark Zuckerberg recently stated that layoffs at Facebook were simply a "course correction from pandemic-era growth and overhiring." His theory of why tech layoffs show no sign of slowing down is that operating a leaner organization is purely "more efficient." There were approximately 11,000 employees let go from Facebook in 2022. I'm confident that many, if not most, of the 11,000 affected were hard workers with solid performance reviews. If anyone thinks there was anything they could have done to save their job, they should be reminded that Zuckerberg said this was merely a course correction for efficiency's sake.

Our emotional struggle isn't a reflection of weakness but of how deeply we invested in our roles and how much we identified with our work. The challenge is finding an equilibrium between the two—acknowledging the harsh logic without invalidating our feelings and moving forward despite the dissonance.

Negotiating a Separation Agreement

Corporate meetings love to provide "leave-behinds." This paperwork is distributed to all in attendance for future reference, even though they typically end up in the small circular filing cabinet on the floor of your office. Layoffs come with their own unique "leave-behind," known as a separation agreement.

While the separation from your job is, unfortunately, non-negotiable, the terms of your release can be negotiated. We negotiate our hiring agreements, why not our separation agreement? Severance pay, health coverage, equipment, references, and referrals may all be on the table. If this is the case, keeping your wits about you is essential. Too often, we agree or sign something the moment it's presented just to move past the pain.

The very nature of an employer-employee relationship is defined by superior-subordinate imbalance. Suddenly, there is an opportunity for equality to be found within the new power dynamic. This idea may be harder to accept for folks in some industries or backgrounds than others. For example, if you're in sales or marketing, you're used to everything being negotiable. I'd imagine that bargaining may not come naturally for those accustomed to the finiteness of accounting or finance. Employers certainly don't want you to think that the terms of your separation are negotiable. Often, a company's initial offer doesn't always reflect the full amount they are willing to pay in severance. So many companies are switching to unlimited PTO not because they've suddenly become very generous but because they no longer have to pay out accrued and unused vacation time upon departure. For many, it's simply a cost-saving measure.

As long as your requests are reasonable, a layoff provides an opportunity to negotiate a fair and equitable separation package that reflects your contributions and circumstances while giving the employer the advantage of a clean break. Perhaps you were let go while six month pregnant; negotiating an extended period of health care coverage would be warranted (and hopefully granted). If your company provided you with a laptop, you can request to keep it to aid with your job search—

I've done this successfully.

Severance pay is often calculated based on tenure: the longer your tenure, the higher the payout. If you've been with the company for five years and they're only putting two weeks on the table, you can and should ask for a larger amount. Suppose the company offers two weeks' severance pay for every year employed, but you'd prefer an extension of health insurance benefits. In that case, you may request to drop to one week of severance each year in exchange for longer insurance coverage. Negotiation isn't just about asking for more; it's about shaping a package that meets your needs while staying aligned with what the company might reasonably provide.

You should be eligible for rehire if you were laid off for reasons unrelated to performance. While strict laws govern what future employers can ask previous employers, they are allowed to ask about your rehire eligibility, assuming their reasons are legitimate and not a pretext for an illegal termination. If the answer is no, it may imply negative connotations, which could discourage a potential employer from extending an offer.

It's essential to understand whether you are eligible for rehire and, if not, the specific reasons. If this is the case, consider focusing your negotiations on securing a classification of "eligible for rehire." Alternatively, you could negotiate for the employer to disclose only your employment dates and last position. Once agreed upon, be sure to get this in writing. You never know when you'll need to provide such documentation as corroboration. Of course, asking for a written recommendation will also serve you well. Getting a prior supervisor to provide a strong recommendation on your LinkedIn profile will go a long way in your search for employment. When in doubt, seek formal legal counsel to understand your rights and options under local employment laws.

With the advent of social media, anonymous company review apps, and platforms like Glassdoor, many companies now include non-disparagement clauses in their separation agreements. It's a relatively unenforceable attempt to prevent former employees from airing the company's "dirty laundry." However, given the influence and reach of sites like Glassdoor, it's clear who's winning the battle.

The key is to ensure that any non-disparagement clause is mutual. This means the company agrees not to say anything negative about you, just as you agree not to say anything negative about them. Again, these clauses are hard to enforce and are unlawful on their face in some states, but having mutual terms in the agreement provides a measure of protection should you get wind of any disparaging remarks down the road.

A helpful reminder: The separation meeting is not the time or place to evaluate their offer and engage in negotiations. It's crucial to process your emotions first before tackling the terms of their proposal. If they give you a short turnaround, ask for more time. For those over age 40, the Older Workers Benefit Protection Act (passed into law by Congress in 1990) legally entitles you to at least 21 days to review the agreement before signing.

Reassure them you are committed to a smooth and successful transition for the company, but prioritize giving yourself ample time to secure the best outcome for your needs. Use this time to carefully review the paperwork, and consider having a lawyer or trusted mentor examine it as well. After understanding their offer, compare it with your original employment agreement. This step will help you confirm your entitlements under the terms of your employment contract and company policies.

If necessary, cross-reference what's included with local employment laws. For instance, a battle is underway with companies' ability to include or enforce non-compete clauses in their employment and severance agreements. As of April 23, 2024, the U.S. Federal Trade Commission voted to ban most non-compete clauses in employer-employee contracts. While the ruling is under appeal at the time of this writing, it is expected to pass. Many states have laws in place that bar such agreements outright, with very limited exceptions. This highlights the importance of researching severance packages for your location, position, industry, and tenure. Conducting thorough due diligence will put you in place to understand what power, leverage, and recourse you have relative to your situation.

Remember: When you sign a severance agreement, you release the company from all past, present, and future liabilities and claims. This legally binding, two-way contract warrants time, consideration, and your strongest counteroffer.

Negotiating in Real Life

Real-world negotiations happen all day, every day. We haggle with service providers over the cost of repairing a leaky roof. We debate with our spouse about who will pick up the kids from school. We wrangle our way out of long-held plans with that irritating neighbor. We counter our friend's ideas about where to go on vacation (beach please).

We are continuously faced with situations where we need to bargain. Some are extreme (like wanting to keep your job), and some less so (like wanting your child to wear a clean shirt to school). Come what may, the subsequent discussions and outcomes largely depend on the emotional intelligence, communication style, and active listening skills of the involved parties.

As such, negotiation situations can go all kinds of ways. What's your default strategy? Are you generally adversarial? Accommodating? Persuasive? The number of tactics at our disposal seem endless, making it worthwhile to reflect on successful, real-world negotiations—not just to appreciate their craft but to understand the skills and techniques that drive results.

In 2013, Walt Disney Company announced its acquisition of Lucasfilm, the behemoth behind the Star Wars franchise, from George Lucas for $4.05 billion. The deal was a surprise to everyone—first that it was even happening, and second that the vastness of terms and provisions had apparently been done amicably, without names being smeared across the front pages. According to Walt Disney Chairman Robert Iger, he and Lucas conducted the negotiations personally for more than two years. Imagine the communication and consideration that went into that!

In early 2021, pharmaceutical company Merck had failed to develop an effective Covid-19 vaccine. When U.S. officials asked the company to help competitor Johnson & Johnson bring *its* vaccine to the public, Merck agreed after the government offered them more than $250 million. Also in 2021, Swiss pharmaceutical firm Novartis and French drugmaker Sanofi helped Pfizer and BioNTech produce their highly effective Covid-19 vaccine. Yes, money talks, but it seems that crisis negotiations can result in rivals working together for the greater good.

In 2022, the U.S. national women's soccer team celebrated an enormous win. That was the year their governing federation agreed to restructure their labor contract. This landmark deal, which took six years of back-and-forth, resulted in a groundbreaking collective bargaining agreement (CBA) that established true pay equity in the sport. Throughout the years of negotiations, the players from the women's soccer team took real ownership of the proceedings and adopted a collaborative approach. They filed legal actions, participated in mediations and hearings, and sat for media interviews as a united front. While tensions undoubtedly arose at times, the women consistently presented as being on the same team, tackling the same issue. All for one, one for all.

The cast of *Friends* famously took this approach as well. After salary disparities emerged during the filming of season three in 1996, all six actors banded together to negotiate equal pay per episode. This meant that two actors would earn less than their current salary, while the other four would see an increase. They made it clear that they would only return if this was agreed upon. NBC ultimately relented, and the six were compensated equally moving forward.

Sixteen years later, six cast members from the sitcom *Modern Family* united similarly when, before production began on the fourth season, the actors sued 20th Century Fox Television to have their contracts voided. When the negotiations ended, all stars received more pay and better benefits and continued to receive substantial raises throughout the remaining seasons of the show.

While these examples are extreme in scale and somewhat irrelevant in our own lives, they share one thing in common: the negotiations were successful largely due to the relational tactics employed. There was a real emphasis on relationship building, solidarity, intention, connection, and trust. Of course, I'm vastly oversimplifying here. It's impossible to know the countless details of what went into those marathon discussions. However, from what we can observe about the processes and results, they serve as extremely positive examples of how to conduct and execute a negotiation.

As you journey through this stage of grief and beyond, remember that negotiations are common in our daily lives—both externally and internally. You will bargain with others and with yourself. But as we've just seen, it never hurts to lean into our humanity. This could mean deploying empathy when dealing with others and practicing self-compassion when dealing with yourself.

The Inevitability of Option B

When Sheryl Sandberg's husband died unexpectedly in 2015, the former COO of Facebook and founder of LeanIn.org navigated the stages of grief publicly and later, in detail, in her book *Option B*.

During the bargaining stage of grief, Sandberg found herself consumed by "what if" and "if only" scenarios, describing an intense sense of guilt, questioning whether there was something she could have done to prevent her husband's death. She also shared how her mind returned again and again to the day her husband passed away, replaying events and asking herself if she had missed any signs. Was there anything she could have done differently that could have saved him? She imagined alternate realities where he was still alive, and they were still building a life together. That was Option A, after all—the life they both wanted and were on track to have. And now that it was gone, she had no choice but to create Option B—let go of "what could have been" and begin to build a path forward.

In the face of unchangeable loss, it's typical to grapple with the unfairness, self-blame, and an overwhelming wish that it could be different. Much like Sandberg shared—and what you may have already gathered from your senseless loss—coming to terms with it often requires scaling the walls we build ourselves. These walls are made out of inferences, culpability, assumptions, and deductions. They're reinforced by conjecture, fault-finding, and answerability. They tower over us, taunting us and prohibiting our growth, resolve, and peace.

We all build walls to protect ourselves, but they can trap us inside instead of allowing us to process, heal, and move forward. In this stage of grief, those walls can feel like a safe haven, yet they often prevent us from seeing new possibilities beyond the loss.

Try to see beyond…what can Option B look like for you?

How To: Advocate For Yourself

When it comes to the literal negotiation following a layoff, most people approach it as a one-way street rather than as an agreement between two equal parties. It's understandable to want to move past the situation quickly, but that doesn't mean you shouldn't use it as an opportunity to advocate for yourself. If that time has already passed, use this as a guide for future situations where you want to seize power and not accept terms at face value.

Knowledge is power in life and in negotiations. Educating yourself thoroughly about the issue and understanding the full scope—from the key facts to the perspectives of those involved —will empower you with a foundation that goes beyond surface-level assumptions. By diving into the specifics, you gain insight into potential obstacles, relevant policies, and practical language to support your case. This preparation clarifies your goals and gives you the confidence to communicate with authority and tact, ultimately positioning you as an informed advocate prepared to engage thoughtfully and strategically.

Practicing assertiveness is another cornerstone of how to advocate for yourself effectively. Assertiveness involves expressing your needs, boundaries, and concerns in a way that is both respectful and confident, helping others understand where you stand without ambiguity. Building this skill can take time and consistent effort, as it requires balancing clarity with composure, even in situations that might be uncomfortable. Through assertive communication, you can strengthen your ability to speak up in a way that garners respect and fosters constructive dialogue. Over time, this approach reinforces your self-assurance and encourages others to respond to you with greater openness and consideration.

If anyone disagrees with your terms, know that it's worthwhile that you tried—if only for the emotional and mental health benefits of self-assertion during a time of vulnerability. There is a satisfaction in metaphorically telling people that you will not go quietly into the night.

Roadmap Exercise: Professional Goals

Once you've acknowledged the reality of the situation and accepted that it wasn't just a mistake and they won't be offering you your job back, it's time to shift your focus to the future.

What do you want for yourself professionally? Plotting career goals can serve as a roadmap for achieving meaningful progress and provide motivation and accountability; knowing what you're working toward can keep you engaged and resilient, even during challenging times.

In your dream professional setting, do you have a leadership role, a remote job, or a role with advancement baked in? What kind of company do you want to work for, and what kind of industry? Do you prefer work culture and perks, or are you more enthusiastic about stock options? How flexible are you with pay, location, or in-office hours? Brainstorm five different non-negotiables and write them in the lines below.

_____

_____

_____

_____

_____

It may be helpful to revisit the North Star exercise from Chapter Two but under the light of what motivates you professionally. When combined with that exercise, your North Star should burn a bit brighter.

Reframe: Focus on What Will Be Next

The path through a layoff is paved with tenacity, resilience, self-care, and a strong belief in oneself. It's easy to let insecurity and self-doubt creep in. Feelings of failure and inadequacy are common. But you have to believe in yourself, and you have to believe that your best days are ahead. Rather than ruminate over what could have been, focus on what will be next.

Stage Four: Depression

Now is when the full weight of this loss can feel heaviest. The past is clouded by what's happened, and the future is uncertain. It's easy to lose your way here, but remember: the night is darkest just before dawn.

Not surprisingly, a 2022 study on the link between depression and unemployment found that 21% of unemployed Americans suffer from depression, compared to only 5.6% of those who work full-time. For those who have been without a job for an extended period—defined as 27 weeks or more—the rate of depression jumps to 28%. A Rutgers University study on long-term unemployment from the same year found that half of the participants experienced shame and embarrassment, causing them to isolate themselves from friends and associates.

Not that you need permission, but it is perfectly normal to feel depressed right now. Financial stress and uncertainty about the future can easily lead to anxiety and feelings of hopelessness under any circumstance. Add to this a sense of rejection, a diminished sense of purpose and self-worth, and you have the formula for a melancholy disposition at best—and full-blown depression at worst.

As if getting laid off weren't hard enough, it likely triggered a chain reaction of destruction. The job loss knocked over the first domino, and then, one by one, each one fell—financial strain, restless days, sleepless nights, sadness, and detachment. For some, this destruction continues until everything is leveled entirely— bankruptcy, divorce, self-harm, or even worse. Take, for example, employees under work visas. The visa allows them to stay in the country while employed, but a layoff means they could face deportation. An immigrant woman was recently let go from X (formerly Twitter) while both six months pregnant and in the process of attaining her green card. As a non-U.S. citizen, the situation left her with two months to leave the country (or find another job) and just one month of health coverage. For her and those like her, the ripple effect from a layoff can truly be catastrophic.

So, could it always be worse? Sure. Does it still feel awful? Yes. You are entitled to a one-person pity party regardless of how many of your dominos fell. It can be an especially dark time if the job you lost was one that you loved. I've found that the more I've loved a job, found purpose in the work, and enjoyed those I worked with, the harder it was to let go. When our identity is linked to our job, and then we lose the job, what follows can be nothing short of an existential crisis.

There was a time when I let my work define me. So often, companies ask you to do the work AND believe wholeheartedly in "The Mission." When done well, it can feel like a community working together toward a shared purpose and common goal. When done poorly, it can feel like a cult. Often led by a very charismatic (aka narcissistic) CEO who serves Kool-Aid whether you're willing to drink it or not, they create an atmosphere where their personality, company vision, and culture are so entwined that it's difficult to tell one from the other. They inflict guilt or shame on any team member who dares to desire a work-life balance—let alone a nine-to-five schedule. And God forbid anyone question the viability of the business plan or product roadmap. Groupthink reigns in these cult-like businesses. "Go along to get along" is the mantra for harmony, but it is the enemy of progress and innovation.

I have found joy, satisfaction, meaning, and purpose from a career in marketing and advertising. Unfortunately, I have also sometimes tied my status and derived self-worth from many jobs. The company's wins were my wins, and their progress was my progress. My co-workers and I were intertwined, our shared goals enough to fuel our sweat equity and skew priorities on the home front. When I was let go, I was devastated. My devotion to the job during my waking hours had meant the slow death of my relationships, hobbies, interests, and life outside of work. In the end, I bet on the wrong thing and lost. It hadn't just become my career identity; I had made it my sole identity.

The Link Between Work and Worth

When we meet new people, one of the first things we're asked is, "What do you do?" When we describe others, it usually includes a mention of their profession. The next-door neighbor is a doctor, an aunt is a software engineer, and a high school friend is an artist. Our identity is inextricably tied to our jobs. It's where we spend most of our time and derive satisfaction. Our job titles, paychecks, and the work we produce become fundamental aspects of how we see ourselves and how others perceive us. This is why a layoff can trigger severe doubts about our self-worth and easily impact our mental health.

To varying degrees, we all derive self-esteem from our jobs. I take a lot of pride and joy in my work accomplishments, accolades, and the awards I've won, as do most of us. According to a recent study, 83% of Americans believe that having a good career is vital to their self-esteem.

A major study by a social scientist at Yale found that work serves three critical functions. First, it provides a degree of economic security (being a "good provider" is, in itself, a mark of self-esteem). Second, it enables independence and eliminates the need for charity or state assistance. Third, and perhaps most importantly, work allows people to feel like they have something to offer; it puts them in the producer role and affirms their worth.

The Yale scientist focused on laid-off workers during the study's second volume. He found that, in most cases, unemployment was followed by frustration and disorganization. Routine decisions led to arguments; everyday chores went unaccomplished; tempers flared. Part of the reason for this was the decreased income; in nearly all cases, any public or private financial aid received was far below the income from the job. But another reason was the elimination of the worker's role of social usefulness. With a job, the worker had somewhere to go each morning, a rhythm to the day. Without work, this rhythm disappeared and was replaced by drifting.

It's important to note that while self-esteem is closely tied to work, not all jobs lead to high self-esteem. Many low-skilled, low-paying, dead-end jobs still exist in our economy, and they don't equate to high self-worth. This raises the question: How does the experience of employment—and potentially, job loss—interact with an individual's self-confidence and past experiences of rejection?

Someone who has experienced any form of rejection before their layoff may have a very different reaction than someone feeling the sting of rejection for the first time. If you have high self-esteem and have never faced rejection, you may coast through your layoff without a second thought. However, if you have low self-esteem and have experienced multiple rejections, this layoff may play right into a pre-existing narrative running on a loop inside your head. For friends who are neurodivergent or have a pre-existing propensity for depression, a layoff can be the spark that ignites a wildfire of self-doubt, anxiety, and despair.

Interestingly, data from the Navy SEAL training program reinforces the significant impact previous experiences with failure can have on resilience. Only about 25% of applicants who start Navy SEAL training successfully graduate and become SEALs. This high attrition rate is due to the famously rigorous demands of BUD/S (Basic Underwater Demolition/SEAL) training, which tests both physical and mental endurance. Research has shown that candidates encountering their first-ever major setbacks during training have higher dropout rates than those who have previously faced and overcome challenges. For instance, star athletes—especially varsity football players or quarterbacks who have never lost a game or thrown an interception in their high school or college careers—often struggle the most when they hit adversity in BUD/S. Accustomed to being the best and excelling at every challenge, these individuals struggle to cope with their first real taste of failure under the intense physical and mental demands of BUD/S, along with the inevitable setbacks it brings.

Since they haven't developed the resilience from overcoming previous setbacks, they're more likely to feel overwhelmed, disheartened, or even question their self-worth. On the other hand, candidates who have faced and recovered from past failures are often better mentally prepared to handle the grueling challenges of BUD/S because they've learned to adapt, persevere, and push through difficulties.

Experiencing setbacks and learning to bounce back are essential elements of resilience and mental toughness—qualities that are critical not only in BUD/S training but also in navigating many of life's challenges, including being laid off.

As someone who has struggled with anxiety and self-esteem issues throughout my life, I've found that when I feed my positive self-esteem with supportive thoughts and experiences, it grows stronger, fostering greater confidence and resilience. This self-reinforcing cycle builds belief in my abilities and encourages me to embrace new challenges and pursue new opportunities. Conversely, my negative self-esteem thrives on criticism, self-doubt, and harsh judgments. When I dwell on my shortcomings, negative thoughts multiply, creating a self-fulfilling prophecy that leads to withdrawal, missed opportunities, and diminished self-worth.

When it comes to self-esteem, the one that grows is the one you feed. For me, starving my depression requires an active, conscious, and daily effort. It often involves choosing to mute the negative feedback loop in my head and replace it with positive self-talk instead.

Separating self-worth from the success or trajectory of our careers can be extraordinarily difficult. Work intricately intersects with our relationships, net worth, and status, making it hard to limit how much our accomplishments—or lack thereof—define us. . Who are we without our job to anchor our identity? For those who allow work to become all-encompassing, this question becomes particularly daunting. Because what happens if you are left without it?

The Importance of Maintaining Balance

Depression is generally caused by a complex cocktail of genetic, biological, environmental, and psychological factors. Regardless of whether you have a pre-existing disposition for depression, a layoff can present easy entry into a deep and dark rabbit hole. And like Alice in Wonderland, once there, it may feel like up is down and down is up.

Layoffs create the ultimate imbalance. Schedules that were once regimented are now open-ended. Self-images, previously fueled by achievement and productivity, become skewed. Bank accounts that once saw regular deposits now reflect uncertainty. So much of our identity is tied to our jobs, and without them, it's like we're in a topsy-turvy new world where normalcy is redefined daily.

When you're ready to reclaim your balance, I suggest starting with your nervous system. The underlying pathophysiological basis of depression is said to be a depletion of the neurotransmitters serotonin, norepinephrine, or dopamine. These neurotransmitters act as chemical messengers in the brain, stimulating feelings of happiness, contentment, and motivation. One nerve cell communicates with another by passing these messages along between brain regions.

Severe and chronic stress, such as that experienced during depression, can disrupt these connections between the nerve cells. The communication within these circuits becomes inefficient and noisy. Researchers believe that the loss of these synaptic connections contributes significantly to the biological basis of depression.

So what to do?

Prescribed medications can be very helpful—and, for some, essential—but there are also many natural ways to support balanced brain chemistry. Lifestyle habits such as regular exercise, quality diets, hot and cold exposure, giving and receiving affection, and spending time outdoors can all increase serotonin and dopamine levels. Fun fact: Serotonin is vital for gut health. Around 95% of this neurotransmitter is produced in the gut, where it interacts with the microbiome.

Maintaining a healthy balance within our body chemistry is imperative, but this principle also extends to everyone's favorite well-being issue: work-life balance. Over nearly 25 years in marketing and advertising, I've rarely encountered anyone who has truly mastered it. Those who came close—establishing clear boundaries with well-defined work hours—often faced setbacks in their careers. Just as prioritizing life over work can hinder professional growth, putting excessive focus on work can have equally harmful effects. However, the answer isn't as simple as achieving a perfect 50/50 split. Instead, the key lies in sustainability.

In both nature and life, everything exists in a dynamic push and pull toward sustainability. From ecosystems to individual organisms, forces like competition, cooperation, and adaptation work ceaselessly to achieve equilibrium. Plants, animals, and even cells seek the resources, energy, and environments needed to maintain stability and foster growth. This pursuit of balance is mirrored in natural cycles—day and night, the changing seasons, life and death—all of which provide renewal and sustain harmony.

The search for sustainability in human life is equally complex, encompassing both physical and psychological dimensions. Our bodies regulate themselves through homeostasis, while our minds seek emotional and social balance. Whether in relationships, work, or personal ambitions, we are constantly adjusting to life's inevitable changes, always striving to find a sense of stability.

Celebrate the opportunity to step back from the relentless hamster wheel of work-life balance. Give yourself permission to pause, take a breath, and reflect on what is truly sustainable in your approach to both work and life. Maybe you can handle 60-hour workweeks with little downtime, or perhaps you may need a rich personal life to fuel your energy for a 40-hour workweek. There is no one-size-fits-all solution, and no one should feel "less than" because of their unique approach to this equation.

Finding balance during this time is crucial to preserving your mental health. Without the structure of a daily job, it's easy to feel like a rudderless ship. Establishing a new routine can provide the foundation for a healthy ecosystem. Effective time management leads to productivity, which, in turn, fosters a sense of purpose. Replacing the community from your job with a new support network will help rebalance that loss. Striking a balance between your job search and activities that boost your serotonin, norepinephrine, and dopamine will allow your brain chemistry to recover from job rejections.

Another way to think about balance is not as a fixed equation but as a continuous flow. Across different points in our lives, we may experience times of intense work focus, while other times call for prioritizing life outside of work. One week, you may be swamped with resumes and job applications; the next, opportunities may feel scarce. Recognize and embrace this flow. Use these ebbs and flows to relax and recharge. Tune into where life is pulling you and where you want to direct your energy. Being mindful and intentional with your focus will help you stay present and more easily notice when depression begins to tug at your mind.

The Bright Side of Being Blue

There's an ongoing debate within the research community about whether depression helps or hinders our cognitive abilities. Some studies suggest that it negatively impacts memory and decision-making, while others propose that depression may actually enhance analytical thinking, particularly when dealing with complex tasks. This combination of findings indicates that depression can sometimes foster a mindset that improves problem-solving in certain situations. Rather than viewing depression solely as detrimental, consider how it may also play a constructive role in specific contexts.

It turns out that when people feel depressed, they often engage in a process called rumination, where they repeatedly dwell on their circumstances. A process also known as "spinning"—of which I am 100% guilty—has long been viewed as a harmful habit that makes it difficult to focus on other things. However, the authors of a study published in *Psychological Review* argue that rumination may actually serve a purpose. They propose the analytical rumination (AR) hypothesis, suggesting that depression could be an evolutionary response to help people zero in on solving tricky problems, rather than getting sidetracked by less important stuff.

According to the hypothesis, depression shifts our focus to urgent problems, enabling us to allocate mental energy more effectively. While this may cause people to lose interest in enjoyable activities—thanks to symptoms like anhedonia, which involves a lack of pleasure or interest in life's experiences—this focused attention is key for addressing complex issues. The idea suggests that when life presents tough challenges, this heightened concentration can lead to a deeper understanding and more effective solutions. So, although it might seem counterintuitive, this process of deep thinking can be beneficial in navigating life's difficulties.

The study is backed by a range of evidence, from genetics to brain function, suggesting that rumination isn't merely a symptom of something gone wrong but may actually be an adaptive trait. The authors challenge the conventional view that depression is solely a mental disorder, proposing instead that it functions as a stress response mechanism that helps us cope with significant life challenges. They advocate for a shift in how we perceive depression—moving beyond the clinical framework to recognize its potential advantages.

Ultimately, we're encouraged to rethink our understanding of depression. By viewing it as an evolved tool for addressing difficult problems, we open the door to a more nuanced perspective that could shape how we approach treatment and support. This shift not only challenges the traditional view of depression as a purely negative state, but also invites us to explore its complexities and potential benefits in facing life's challenges. At the very least, this alternative perspective may allow you to extend some grace to yourself on those particularly difficult days.

How To: Practice Self-Care

The whole idea of self-care has come a long way. Our nation's focus on personal health and well-being surged in the late 1960s and 1970s, driven by social movements like vegetarianism, natural health, and aerobic exercise. What once existed on the fringe of pop culture quickly became central to it, moving from casual public conversation to deliberate public consumption. As the decades passed, so too did our evolving commitment to maintaining our health in mind, body, and spirit. Today, self-care is not just an acceptable practice—it's critical for keeping the depressive demons at bay.

You might think I'm referring to spa days and complicated skin-care routines, but self-care is more than just self-indulgence or instant gratification—it's also about setting yourself up for future success. What separates many of the world's most successful individuals from the rest is how they approach self-care: they make choices in the moment that improve their lives down the line.

This could mean getting enough sleep, eating healthy, building a supportive social network, or exploring a hobby that brings you joy—things that accumulate and help fend off depression over time. But let's take it a step further. What if self-care also looked like tackling that sink full of dishes, completing the workout you keep postponing, or checking off the most daunting items on your to-do list? You know, those things that aren't particularly fun at the moment but feel incredibly satisfying once completed.

Mark Twain once said, "If it's your job to eat a frog, eat it first thing in the morning. And if it's your job to eat two frogs, eat the bigger one first." This speaks to the power of tackling your most challenging or unpleasant tasks first. By doing so, you set yourself up for increased productivity and a sense of accomplishment throughout the day.

By "eating the frog," you eliminate procrastination and create momentum for tackling other tasks. Research shows that everyday tasks like loading the dishwasher or hanging out laundry can actually boost happiness if approached mindfully. In one study, volunteers were encouraged to view dishwashing as an opportunity of mindfulness—focusing on the present moment and the sensation of the warm water and suds. After just six minutes of washing, participants reported feeling 27% less anxious and 25% more inspired.

I get it if you'd prefer a 90-minute massage over eating a frog. Enjoying life is non-negotiable. However, it's important to also recognize the satisfaction that comes from progress. Each small accomplishment and item crossed off your to-do list brings you one step closer to where you want to be.

Roadmap Exercise: Pursue Joy

In Chapter Two, I introduced the concept of a personal North Star and suggested a framework for achieving personal goals (running a marathon, for example). I invite you now to revisit those guiding principles from a new perspective. Take inventory of the things in your life that bring you joy. Think of this as the Marie Kondo method of decluttering your closet—but instead, apply it to life. If something sparks joy, seek it out and make time for it. Rinse and repeat. The best way to battle depression and sadness is by pursuing joy.

Use the lines below to identify what fills your cup. What recharges your batteries? What activities do you genuinely look forward to? Aim to discover something that replenishes your mind (reading a book), body (engaging in regular exercise), and spirit (establishing a gratitude practice). What activities will elevate your serotonin and dopamine levels? Maybe social settings and community interactions are sources of joy for you. If that's the case, create weekly appointments for coffee or dinner with friends.

Don't hesitate to include guilty pleasures as well. Watching reality TV might be just the escape you need from your own reality. This is about finding your happiness—without shame or guilt.

_____

_____

_____

_____

_____

_____

Reframe: There Is a Crack in Everything, That's How the Light Gets In

An ancient Japanese art called _kintsugi_ translates to "mend with gold." In this practice, artists repair broken ceramics and pottery using gold lacquer, transforming the pieces into something even more striking and unique than before they were broken. Philosophically, _kintsugi_ treats breakage and repair as integral to the object's history rather than something to be hidden. The beauty of the art rests in the truth that vessels are more magnificent _because_ of their imperfections, not in spite of them. As you move through your layoff, you may feel tempted to conceal or hide this experience from others. I encourage you to do the opposite. The only way to overcome the shame and embarrassment associated with layoffs is to be loud and proud. By embracing your story, you may find kinship with the 40% of Americans who have faced a layoff themselves.

Additional Support

The severity and degree to which you experience depression as a result of your layoff will vary. One day it may come, and another day it could go. For some, it may come and never leave. It may be very severe, and nothing written here seems useful. Fortunately, there are more mental health resources available today than ever before. Below are just a few; please reach out if you find yourself struggling or need support navigating these challenging feelings. Remember, you're not alone, and help is within reach.

Suicide Hotline: dial 988
Depression and Bipolar Support Alliance: visit
www.dbsalliance.org
Simple way to find an ideal therapist: go to www.zencare.co
Be kind to your mind: www.headspace.com

Stage Five: Acceptance

The journey, until now, has felt like a struggle between the push and pull of comfort, peace, and the grief associated with denial, pain, and depression. The tug-of-war between these forces has certainly grown tiresome and defeating. Acceptance is when we drop the rope. We accept our circumstances and stop resisting by letting go. The only way to win is to walk away from the fight. This doesn't mean we condone or approve of the situation; it simply means we stop expending energy on fighting against things we cannot change.

In the early 1930s, American theologian Reinhold Niebuhr wrote the Serenity Prayer, which has been adopted by many 12-step programs as a source of wisdom for personal strength through acceptance. The prayer begins as an address to God, but many replace this with a more flexible and inclusive term, such as "Higher Power." You can insert or remove whichever term suits your preference. The important thing is not the identity of God, but rather the wisdom found in the sentiment.

God, grant me the serenity to accept the things I cannot change,
Courage to change the things I can,
And wisdom to know the difference.

Acceptance does not negate the negative experience, nor is it a fast pass to joy. It is an acknowledgment of the pain and loss you have experienced. It's not about "moving on," but accepting and weaving what has happened into your new reality and identity. This experience will become part of who you are. I invite you to view it through the lens of growth and resilience. I won't go as far as to say that being laid off is a "character-building experience"— I'd probably react unfavorably if anyone ever said that to me. What I'm suggesting is that accepting the layoff can cultivate a mindset better prepared to handle future challenges or setbacks, helping to foster a belief in one's ability to overcome adversity and adapt.

As mentioned earlier, you may experience many different stages of grief on the same day. This journey isn't a one-way street that only allows forward progress. Everyone's road to acceptance is unique, and some emotions may linger longer than others. For instance, you may still grapple with depression while navigating your course to acceptance. We already know that the secret to managing the stages of grief is through a whole-body approach— mind, body, and spirit. A key to positive mental health is reframing the experience. Job loss isn't a dead end; it's a detour to something else. It's up to you to define what that next thing is. Managing a positive mindset and attitude is the route through the obstacle. Instead of viewing setbacks as failures, consider them as opportunities for growth and learning.

If I could identify one difference between my first layoff in 2001 and my last in 2023, it would be my mindset. I viewed my first layoff as a giant personal failure that took years to recover from. I couldn't reframe the experience as a growth opportunity; I saw it only as an unfair situation happening to me. For exercise, I would run on the hamster wheel of "what ifs," preventing me from making any progress because I was focused on the past. Fast forward to 2023, and not only did I accept my layoff as an unfortunate but necessary part of the business world, but I also saw it as a redirection to something else. Instead of asking "what if," I directed my attention to "what next."

In Buddhism, there's a common metaphor comparing a rock and a stream to illustrate the principles of resilience and acceptance. Essentially, the rock stubbornly sits in the middle of a flowing stream, and as time passes, the stream gently shapes the rock. The rock represents rigid thinking, attachment to fixed ideas, and resistance to life's changes. The stream, on the other hand, represents flexibility and acceptance. Instead of resisting obstacles, the stream adapts its path around them.

In 2001, I was the rock. Twenty-two years later, I was the stream. Job loss can feel like the rock in the middle of life's stream—a sudden, immovable obstacle that feels impossible to move past. At first, it's tempting to be like the rock, clinging to anger, resistance, or attachment to what was. However, finding acceptance allows us to become more like the stream. Instead of pushing against what cannot be changed, we learn to adapt and flow around it. By accepting the reality of job loss, we create space for new opportunities and possibilities to emerge, enabling ourselves to move forward and gradually shape a new path, just as the stream does over time.

Mindset Shift: Radical Acceptance

Acceptance is a central Buddhist concept: it encourages understanding and peaceful coexistence with life's inevitable changes and challenges. In the late 1980s and early 1990s, American psychologist Dr. Marsha Linehan combined this Eastern philosophical principle with Cognitive Behavioral Therapy (CBT) to develop Dialectical Behavior Therapy (DBT). One key component of DBT is radical acceptance, which is now widely recognized in mental health and personal growth fields. It is being applied beyond DBT in practices like trauma recovery, stress management, and general well-being practices.

Radical acceptance involves acknowledging what cannot be changed, letting go of the need to control outcomes, and embracing emotions, thoughts, and circumstances as they are. Sounds a little like the Serenity Prayer, doesn't it? But that's where the radical part comes in.

The concept asks us to embrace reality *completely* and *wholeheartedly*, without resistance—even when it's painful or unfair. Rather than having a neutral or detached stance, like an "it is what it is" attitude, radical acceptance requires a deep emotional acknowledgment and the willingness to let go of judgment and resentment. This mindset shift demands a deliberate effort to reframe how we engage with our emotions and the challenges we face. By fully confronting our feelings, we stop the mental fight against reality and can find our way from pain to peace.

The crux of this idea is to let go of our perceptions of how things should be for an acceptance of how things are. By releasing unrealistic expectations, we free up mental and emotional energy necessary for healing. When we hope that situations—or people, for that matter—will change, we remain tethered to the idea that things could be different. Once freed of this anchor, you will discover the release of acceptance.

In the face of job loss, radical acceptance might look like someone saying, "This is painful and difficult, but it has happened, and I can face it." They allow themselves to feel sadness, frustration, and even fear, but instead of resisting these emotions, they embrace them without trying to alter the reality of the situation. Radical acceptance helps reduce additional emotional suffering from trying to deny or argue with reality. It can help break the cycle of "what if" thinking, where we dwell on things we could have done differently to keep our job.

Instead of thinking, "If only I had worked harder," radical acceptance shifts the mindset to, "This happened, and while I wish things were different, I accept that this is the reality now." Letting go of regrets opens the door to moving forward.

Carl Rogers, a renowned American psychologist, once said, "The curious paradox is that when I accept myself just as I am, then I can change." Similarly, Carl Jung, the founder of analytic psychology, said, "What you resist not only persists but will grow in size." These ideas underscore a critical truth, particularly in the face of a job loss: resisting difficult emotions often exacerbates suffering. And if those quotes from two psychologists named Carl are too lofty, I offer something more succinct. As The Borg Collective from Star Trek famously said, "Resistance is futile."

Acceptance as an Emotion Regulation Strategy

In a recent study published in *Frontiers in Psychology,* researchers examined acceptance as an emotional regulation strategy. While most of us are familiar with the concept of emotional regulation, the degree to which we practice it varies greatly. Effectively managing our responses to emotionally challenging experiences is crucial for personal growth and emotional resilience. Certain situations may trigger stronger reactions than others, just as certain people may trigger more intense reactions. Throughout the day, we react to stressors and cope with them. Depending on the situation, we may use different strategies in an attempt to respond appropriately. Our reactions shape how we cope with stress, either in healthy or unhealthy ways.

When negative emotions arise, we can talk with friends, exercise, meditate, or take a few deep breaths. Alternatively, we may choose less healthy coping mechanisms, like abusing alcohol, overeating, or engaging in physical aggression. We've all been guilty of resorting to less-than-ideal emotional regulation strategies at times. For many of us—including myself—responding to stressful situations in a healthy way requires unlearning old habits and consciously adopting new ones.

So, what makes emotions feel so overwhelming? It's important to recognize that the experience of an emotion itself doesn't cause difficulty; it's our *interpretation* and *reaction* to the emotion that often creates challenges. If left unchecked, our thoughts, feelings, and behavior can become trapped in a vicious cycle.

For example, consider this common scenario: a friend walks past you without acknowledgement. You might immediately feel a rush of emotions—confusion, disappointment, self-doubt, or even anger. These feelings quickly spark thoughts like, "Did I do something wrong?" or "Maybe she's mad at me for something that happened a while back." Even if you try to brush it off, convincing yourself that you're overreacting, the initial emotional response can lead to more intense feelings like frustration or insecurity. This discomfort often drives you to act—whether by overthinking, avoiding the friend, or distracting yourself with something comforting. Before you know it, you're caught in a pattern where your emotions and reactions feed off each other.

If the cycle continues unchecked, avoiding those uncomfortable feelings only fuels more negative thoughts and emotions, reinforcing your initial interpretation of the event. You might start thinking, "Our friendship is falling apart," or even worry about losing more friends. Over time, what began as a small moment can escalate into a much larger reaction, especially if it taps into past narratives or deeper fears. This cycle can become even harder to break when the triggering event is more intense or tied to unresolved trauma.

I'll admit that I've developed a rather unhealthy coping strategy as a result of having been laid off four times. After the first experience of being given only a few minutes to put my personal belongings in a box before being escorted out of the building, I became reluctant to bring personal items to an office. I can still hear Rober DeNiro's character from *Heat* saying, "Don't let yourself get attached to anything you are not willing to walk out on in 30 seconds flat if you feel the heat around the corner." Since then, I've made sure I had nothing in my office that couldn't be packed away in under a minute. One unexpected benefit of working from home is that if you're laid off over Zoom, you don't need to endure the humiliation of packing your things in front of coworkers with security suspiciously watching over your shoulder. However, the byproduct of this strategy of detachment went beyond the physical items I kept in my workspace—it also spilled over into my ability to develop close relationships with coworkers, whether I worked from home or in-office.

Instead of avoiding attachment, acceptance would encourage me to acknowledge my feelings of vulnerability without letting them control me. By allowing myself to process these emotions in a more rational and healthy way, I could face the challenge of developing closer bonds with coworkers without the fear of being hurt. This approach would help me build emotional resilience, while fostering the flexibility needed to engage more meaningfully with others.

What sets acceptance apart from other emotional regulation strategies is that it doesn't attempt to change or suppress emotions. Rather, it encourages us to let them exist without interference. By accepting emotions as they arise, I can avoid the urge to overanalyze or react impulsively. This shift in perspective would be transformative in helping me process my feelings more effectively, face the challenge of forming close relationships with coworkers, and heal from the fear of future loss. Rather than resisting attachment, acceptance would allow me to acknowledge and experience vulnerability without letting it dictate my actions, cultivating emotional resilience and enabling deeper connections.

I recognize that changing our thoughts is much easier than changing our feelings, especially when there is considerable emotional baggage to unpack.

The Art of Noble Lessons

In 2000, Sara Blakely created Spanx with just $5,000. Today, she is one of the youngest self-made female billionaires, known for her innovative approach to business. She's been included in *Time* magazine's list of the 100 most influential people in the world, and in 2014, *Forbes* listed her as the 93rd most powerful woman. However, her journey is far from a linear success story. She faced numerous setbacks and failures, but her resilience and adaptability helped her turn obstacles into opportunities.

Initially, Blakely aspired to follow in her father's footsteps and become a lawyer, but after failing the LSAT not once, but twice, she realized law school was not her path. She worked various odd jobs, including at Disney World, doing stand-up comedy, and spending seven years selling fax machines door-to-door in the Florida heat. It was during that time that she came up with the idea for Spanx as an alternative to pantyhose. Despite having zero experience in fashion or manufacturing and facing numerous rejections, she persevered. It may not be surprising that the hosiery mills were largely dominated by men who didn't understand the innovative product Blakely was offering. So why did she continue to pursue this idea after so many setbacks? When asked, Blakely attributes her persistence to advice she received from her father at a young age. Rather than asking about her grades or how many goals she scored in soccer, he would ask, "What did you fail at this week?" He would be disappointed if she had nothing to report and would give her a high five when she shared what she tried and failed.

In an interview for *Fortune* magazine, she said, "I didn't realize at the time how much of this advice would define not only my future but my definition of failure...so many people don't pursue their ideas because they're scared or afraid of what could happen. My dad taught me that failing simply leads you to the next great thing."

This mindset taught Blakely to redefine failure—not as not achieving the desired outcome, but as not trying at all. While I am not suggesting that being laid off should be associated with failure, I use this anecdote to emphasize the value of strength and perseverance in overcoming life's challenges. Resilience is the backbone of adapting to difficulties in a healthy way. It involves mental flexibility, positivity, and the capacity to manage stress—qualities essential for building a business and rebuilding a career post-layoff. Resilience is about bouncing back.

Grit, on the other hand, combines passion and perseverance toward long-term goals, even in the face of setbacks. It's a commitment to keep going, no matter the obstacles. Unlike resilience, which focuses on recovery, grit is about persistence and dedication over time.

What if we viewed setbacks as opportunities? What if we saw life's roadblocks as serendipitous detours? What if we embraced failure as a noble lesson in its own right?

How To: Practice Gratefulness

Gratitude doesn't always come easily during difficult times, but it is a skill that can be developed through intention and consistency. Cultivating a daily practice helps shift your focus toward what is positive and meaningful, gradually rewiring your brain to notice and savor uplifting experiences more readily. This, in turn, fosters a greater sense of well-being and resilience.

Start by writing down three things you're grateful for at the end of each day. These could be as simple as a supportive conversation with a friend, a comforting meal, or the strength to take a deep breath and keep moving forward. Practicing gratitude doesn't mean dismissing the hard parts of your journey; it's about creating space to appreciate what is still good.

Next, consider extending gratitude to the positive aspects of your former job or employer. Perhaps you gained valuable skills, forged meaningful relationships, or benefited from a mentor's guidance. Maybe there's a sense of pride in a project you completed or relief in a reasonable severance package. Even if your departure was unexpected or painful, finding gratitude in these moments allows you to reframe the experience and carry forward the parts that served you well.

Lastly, express gratitude for the possibilities ahead. While transitions often come with uncertainty, they also provide a chance to reassess your goals and dreams. Be thankful for the space to explore what you truly want in the next chapter of your life. This mindset doesn't require having all the answers; it's about embracing the unknown with curiosity and optimism. Shifting your focus from loss to potential fosters hope and empowerment as you move forward.

Roadmap Exercise: Strengths and Weaknesses

Every experience—especially challenging ones—reveals what we're truly capable of. Identifying our strengths and areas for growth is essential for both professional and personal development. By understanding where we excel, we can leverage those strengths to overcome obstacles and maximize our potential. At the same time, acknowledging our weaknesses opens the door to growth, enabling us to refine areas that may hold us back and create a more balanced, empowered version of ourselves.

Take a moment to reflect on the challenges you've been navigating and identify at least five strengths that have supported you along the way. These might include skills like problem-solving, traits such as discipline, or core values like honesty. Write them down as a reminder of the qualities you've relied on and demonstrated throughout this journey.

_____

_____

_____

_____

_____

_____

Next, consider five areas where you see room for improvement or growth. These might involve behaviors such as procrastination, habits like negative self-talk, or skills such as delegation. Approach this exercise with kindness and curiosity—it's about discovery, not self-criticism.

_____

_____

_____

_____

_____

_____

Progress requires honest reflection and a willingness to be vulnerable. Embrace the process of growth with patience, understanding that both strengths and weaknesses are essential aspects of your unique journey. Growth is rarely linear; it's about taking consistent small steps toward becoming the best version of yourself. By continuously reflecting and identifying areas for improvement, you create opportunities to evolve, adapt, and thrive.

Reframe: Acceptance Is an Acknowledgment of the Truth

Acceptance is the recognition of reality. It allows us to confront the truth of a situation without the weight of denial or resistance. By acknowledging circumstances as they are, we create space for clarity and the potential for growth, instead of exhausting ourselves by battling against the unchangeable. This perspective empowers us to make informed decisions and take meaningful actions. Acceptance isn't about giving up; it's about seeing things as they truly are and responding with wisdom, not frustration or despair

Stage Six: Reconstruction

Like a phoenix rising from the ashes, reconstruction is when we reassemble the pieces and emerge stronger from the experience. The journey through a layoff is rife with personal, professional, and financial challenges—it's a crucible that transforms weaknesses and reveals strengths. It shines a light on our priorities, career path, and purpose. The person you were before a layoff is unlikely to be the same person you become after it.

Without exception, I emerged from every layoff stronger than I was before. Each layoff taught me valuable lessons about resilience and grit. At times, it took a while for those lessons to become clear, but eventually, I came to realize that I wasn't a victim of my circumstances—I was the architect of my response to them. Reconstruction is about asking yourself, "What actions do I need to take to build a new life for myself?"

An ancient Greek myth involves the legendary ship of the hero Theseus, which was preserved in Athens as a symbol of his victories. Over time, the wooden planks of the ship began to decay. To maintain the ship, each plank was replaced with an identical new one until none of the original wood remained. Herein lies the Greek philosophical thought experiment: Is the reconstructed ship still the same as the Ship of Theseus? If the ship has none of its original parts, can it still be considered the same object? What if the old, decaying wood was used to build another ship? Which of the two would be the true Ship of Theseus—the one with the new planks or the one rebuilt with the old planks?

Experiencing a layoff can feel like losing key components of your identity, much like the ship's planks being replaced. Your job may have been a core part of who you were—personally, professionally, or financially. In the reconstruction stage, you will begin replacing the "planks" of your life. This might include developing new skills, pursuing further education, and reevaluating personal values and priorities. You may find satisfaction in your current career path and decide to double down, or you may choose to change your career trajectory. There are no wrong answers.

As you reconstruct your life, you may wonder if you're still the same person without your old job or if you still bring the same value to the table. The answer, not unlike the answer to the Ship of Theseus thought experiment, lies in recognizing that your core essence, skills, passions, and experiences remain intact, even as your external circumstances change. Your knowledge, talents, and abilities don't disappear just because you were laid off. Like the new wooden planks, reconstruction doesn't erase the past; it integrates it into a stronger, more purposeful future.

When Janice from Human Resources looks at my resume, she won't see a steady climb up the corporate ladder. What she will likely see is more of a romp across a playground jungle gym. Some positions may seem lateral, while others are in entirely different industries. Some are short-lived, and others are longer in duration. She may see someone who is not risk-averse and possibly someone unafraid to pivot. However, it's more likely that Janice won't even see my resume, because she will likely run it through an Applicant Tracking System (ATS). If you're unfamiliar with ATS, it's an AI-enabled software system where resumes go to die. The reality is that most resumes are more like mine than those resembling Sir Edmund Hillary's slow but sure climb up the corporate mountain.

During one of my involuntary work hiatuses, I looked at the trends shaping the marketing industry. I saw a new category emerging as marketing shifted from generalist roles to more specific vertical skill sets. The rise of the Software as a Service (SaaS) industry created a demand for new skills. Niche marketing expertise became highly sought after, fueled by the widespread adoption of cloud computing, which made software solutions more accessible, scalable, and affordable. Marketing efforts for SaaS products increasingly focused on consumer benefits and the product's overall value proposition—hence the birth of Product Marketing. As I was on the job hunt, I saw a lot of openings for Product Marketers. It seemed as if many of the marketing jobs that were being eliminated were being replaced by Product Marketing positions. As I read these job descriptions, I thought: (1) I can totally do this, and (2) these jobs sound pretty exciting. With a little nip and tuck to my resume, I could highlight my applicable experience to prospective employers and take advantage of the job openings in this growing industry. After a long and successful career in advertising and marketing, I used this as an opportunity to reposition and reframe skill sets in a way that allowed my experience to remain relevant.

Reconstruction is a time to regain your footing, reset boundaries, realign your skills, reprioritize your values, and reclaim your career. Asking, "What can life look like from here?" is an opportunity not just to begin a job search, but to envision a future that matches your purpose and passion.

Unlike the initial phases of anger or denial, reconstruction is marked by a subtle shift from the intense emotions of loss to practical steps and problem-solving. The sting of losing your job may still linger, but now there's a growing sense of clarity. You begin looking at the future with a more grounded mindset, assessing what actions are needed to navigate this new chapter. At this point, the journey transitions from reflection to intentional action.

Rebounding Through Resilience

A well-known Japanese proverb says, "Fall seven times, stand up eight." This statement embodies resilience, perseverance, and determination to overcome obstacles. It suggests that no matter how many times life knocks you down, what truly matters is your ability to keep getting back up, stronger and more determined than before. Get laid off once, twice, three, or four times? Stand up five.

Being laid off from a job is a profoundly difficult experience, but like all difficult experiences, it provides an opportunity for growth. Now is the time to reflect and gain clarity. Embrace this moment as a chance to reimagine your future. Consider everything you've learned, what you've enjoyed, and what has challenged you in previous roles. Examine your successes and the skills that come naturally to you. As mentioned, it's essential to separate the layoff from your sense of self-worth. Remember, layoffs are often driven by external factors like restructuring or economic changes, not your abilities. Use this time of introspection to clarify your priorities and redefine the type of work and environment that aligns with your values and strengths.

As you move forward, reconnect with your sense of purpose. Reflect on what truly motivates you and explore how your next role can align with that passion. Many people find that a layoff pushes them toward opportunities they wouldn't have considered otherwise—ones that better match their values or long-term vision.

Building resilience is key to navigating this transition. Instead of viewing the layoff as a setback, consider it an opportunity to reset, rebuild, and create a stronger foundation for your career. Set small, achievable goals, like updating your résumé, contacting your network, or preparing for job interviews. When discussing your layoff with prospective employers, you must frame it positively. Share how the experience has allowed you to enhance your skills, expand your perspective, and emerge with a clearer sense of direction. It's imperative to frame this time as a period of growth, not as a soul-crushing experience that has drained both your bank account and self-esteem. While true, Janice isn't interested in honest answers such as these during the job interview process. Besides, giving oxygen to the positive aspects will help feed a narrative that emphasizes the benefits rather than the negatives, of which there are plenty to choose. Remember, the one that grows is the one that's fed.

If there's one piece of advice worth the price of this book, it's this: Above all else, find a circle of friends that will help you see the humor in this experience. Friends who help you turn tears into laughter are the best kind. They foster resilience. Resilience isn't forged from the fire of anger; it grows from the ability to accept challenges with positivity, adaptability, and joy. And sometimes, sarcasm…

While uncertainty can be uncomfortable, it's also where growth happens. Resilience means acknowledging the challenges while staying focused on the bigger picture of what lies ahead. Each step forward, no matter how small, is progress. Ultimately, being laid off can become a catalyst for transformation, allowing you to build a career that not only aligns with your skills but is also driven by a more profound sense of purpose and fulfillment.

"It is not the strongest of the species that survives, nor the most intelligent, but the one most responsive to change." This often misrepresented quote from Charles Darwin emphasizes that adaptability to changing conditions is the key factor in survival. All things can—and do—change. Happy with the weather? Just wait, it will change. Happy with your job? Just wait, it will change. Happy in your relationship? Just wait, it will change. The only thing certain in this life, besides death (and taxes), is change. Seeing change as an opportunity is the secret to personal growth. In *Pivot: The Only Move That Matters Is Your Next One*, Jenny Blake writes, "Maintaining a growth mindset is critical to navigating a pivot successfully. By seeing change as an opportunity rather than a personal shortcoming or obstacle, you will be much more likely to find creative solutions based on what excites you rather than subpar choices clouded by fear."

A growth mindset views obstacles as opportunities to grow rather than as threats. It treats failures as temporary setbacks and part of the learning process. People with a growth mindset are more likely to take risks, embrace lifelong learning, and achieve higher levels of fulfillment. For example, a student with a growth mindset struggling with math would tell themselves, "I don't understand this yet, but with practice, I'll get better." Similarly, someone who struggles with public speaking would say, "I can become a better speaker with practice and feedback." This optimism for change fosters a belief that future improvement is possible, even if things are difficult now.

A growth mindset primarily looks forward into the future, but it also thoughtfully looks backward to learn from past experiences. Similarly, the rearview mirror is smaller than the windshield because where you're going is more important than where you've been.

Ultimately, we are not victims of our circumstances; we are defined by how we respond to our challenges. Losing a job doesn't strip away your ability to determine what comes next. Success and failure are subjective—you, not anyone else, define them. Your dignity is yours to hold onto, no matter what happens. No one can take it unless you let them. The same is true for hope and pride—they remain yours if you keep them alive. Your skills, creativity, and imagination are still with you; they're powerful tools, but they only matter if you choose to use them. The real challenge isn't the setback; it's deciding how to rebuild and keep going.

The Power of Pivoting

In the reconstruction stage, examining the gaps in your resume and the openings in your chosen field or industry is an essential exercise for determining the size or scope of a possible career pivot. Your job function may be in high demand, so a pivot into something different may not be necessary. Alternatively, this could be an opportunity to acquire new skills in an adjacent arena. For others, this may be the perfect time to pause and dive deeper into their life's purpose for a more seismic shift.

There are many ways to look at career pivots. Shipping tankers are massive vessels that require significant time and distance to change direction due to their size, momentum, and the limitations of their steering systems. Unlike a car, which can quickly make a sharp turn, a shipping tanker must adjust its course incrementally, often taking miles to execute even a moderate turn. Like this metaphor of a shipping tanker making gradual turns, I made a subtle turn toward Product Marketing. However, some may find their pivot needs to be more swift and dramatic.

We live in a time of dynamic change and extraordinary possibilities. It's common to hear stories about the laid-off accountant who started a successful bakery or the copywriter who developed a renowned new software application. Career pivots can be acts of rediscovery—an intentional choice to leverage existing skills in new ways or to embrace entirely different roles. It's a time to evaluate long-held ambitions, reconnect with passions that may have taken a backseat, and consider fresh possibilities that align more closely with your values. Pivoting isn't about abandoning experience—it's about reimagining how it can serve a new purpose and lead to a more fulfilling direction.

Take the example of a woman born in the late 1940s in New York. For as long as she could remember, she dreamed of gliding across the ice, a vision of grace and strength. She trained relentlessly, competing in figure skating at the highest levels. But despite her passion and discipline, she didn't make the Olympic team. It was devastating, but she didn't dwell on it for long. She pivoted to a new dream, trading her skates for a desk at *Vogue*. For 17 years, she poured her heart into fashion journalism, working her way up the ranks, sure she was destined to become editor-in-chief. But when the promotion came up, it didn't go to her. Once again, she was left standing on the sidelines, wondering if she was chasing the wrong dream.

At 40 years old, most would have said it was too late to start over, but she didn't see it that way. Inspired by her search for a wedding dress, she decided to try designing her own. With no formal training, she created a modern, elegant, bold gown unlike anything else on the market. That single dress sparked a new passion and a new career. Within a few years, her designs became synonymous with luxury, redefining bridal fashion and dressing celebrities on red carpets worldwide. Today, Vera Wang is one of the most celebrated designers in the world, proving that success doesn't always come on the first—or even the second—try.

Another example is an Indiana-born man with a steady job, a good paycheck, and a comfortable routine. Life wasn't glamorous, but it was secure. For nearly 20 years, he worked at the same automotive plant, clocking in and out daily, ensuring parts met quality standards. He never dreamed of doing anything else. But one gray November morning, the plant manager called everyone into the breakroom. The company was shutting down, and all the jobs were gone.

At 45, he was jobless and unsure of what to do next. He tried applying for work at other factories, but no one was hiring. Weeks turned into months, and desperation began to creep in. Until one night, while trying to save money, he decided to make dinner for his family—a fried chicken recipe he had perfected over the years. His family raved about it, just like they always had. And then his daughter asked, "Why don't you sell this, Dad?"

The idea seemed ridiculous at first. He wasn't a chef and knew nothing about running a business. But he was out of options. Using his last paycheck, he bought a few ingredients and started cooking his famous chicken from his tiny kitchen, selling meals to neighbors. Word spread quickly. Soon, he couldn't keep up with demand. He rented a small space, then a bigger one, and then partnered with investors to open his first restaurant.

By the time he was 60, his Kentucky fried chicken recipe wasn't just known in his neighborhood—it was known across the country, and Colonel Harland Sanders became a household name.

I could go on ad nauseam with examples of people who pivoted into something new. Ina Garten worked in the White House Office of Management and Budget before opening a specialty food store and becoming known as the "Barefoot Contessa." Jack Ma was an English and international trade lecturer before founding Alibaba, China's version of Amazon. Ray Kroc was a World War I ambulance driver, real estate agent, and salesman for a paper cup company before purchasing McDonald's and revolutionizing the fast-food industry. Oprah Winfrey was famously told she was "unfit for television." Steve Jobs was fired from Apple. Walt Disney was told he "lacked imagination."

What do all these stories have in common? They all rebuilt and kept going.

Psychologically speaking, career pivots are attempts to align our occupational choices with our self-concept or identity. Whether driven by a desire for a greater purpose, work-life balance, or industry shifts, deciding to pivot can allow you to break free from stagnation and stay adaptable in an ever-changing workforce. Pivoting offers the opportunity to step into new industries or roles, transforming your route from monotonous to scenic. While the idea of career pivoting can seem daunting, remember that it doesn't mean starting from scratch! You can confidently enter more fulfilling and dynamic roles by leveraging existing skills and experience while acquiring new knowledge.

Mentally Preparing Yourself for The Great Unknown

In 1817, poet John Keats introduced the concept of negative capability, which he described as the ability to remain in uncertainties, mysteries, and doubts without striving for clear answers or logical explanations. During the aftermath of a job loss, embracing Keats's concept offers a profound approach to navigating this challenging period. His notion emphasizes how growth often requires tolerance for ambiguity and a willingness to sit with unresolved questions. For those facing a layoff, this mindset means embracing the unknown without rushing to find immediate answers or a clear path forward. Instead of searching for rational explanations for why the job loss happened or what comes next, negative capability encourages acceptance of ambiguity, creating space for a more open and flexible recovery process.

This approach also means focusing on the present rather than being consumed by regrets over the past or anxiety about the future. By resisting the urge to analyze every detail, you allow yourself to fully experience each step of the recovery process, managing emotions constructively instead of spiraling into unproductive thought patterns. In that openness lies the potential for reinvention—a chance to explore new creative directions, career paths, or skills you hadn't previously considered. Negative capability reframes this reconstruction period as an opportunity where growth arises from sitting comfortably in the unknown, trusting that discovery will come in its own time.

Eighteen months. That's how long it took me to find another job after I was laid off in March of 2001. During that time, my wife and I simultaneously faced deep uncertainty in the aftermath of each of our layoffs, along with many others in San Francisco. It's estimated that five million people nationwide lost their jobs due to the unexpected implosion of so many companies. Particularly hard-hit were those in the nascent technology industry.

I found the job market in Los Angeles was less impacted by the dot-com crash, and after seeing so many jobs eliminated in the Bay Area seemingly overnight, we decided to take action. That summer, we packed up and moved to sunny Southern California, hoping for a fresh start. I found it encouraging when it was difficult to locate a U-Haul—so many others seemed to have the same idea, confirming that our decision might be a good one. While this wasn't entirely accurate, it did feel like the entire city was leaving. The new gold rush that brought everyone to this great city had ended, and now everyone was leaving for their next opportunity.

Initially, it felt promising. My wife went back to college full-time, and I threw myself into applying and interviewing for jobs. We missed San Francisco but remained optimistic. Then, September 11 happened, compounding what was already a fragile job market. Overnight, the few warm leads I had disappeared. Interviews were canceled. The sense of possibility we had clung to slipped away, leaving nothing but uncertainty.

This is where I learned the true essence of negative capability—sitting in the discomfort of what felt unknowable and unresolved. Looking back at my decision to leave San Francisco was easy, but it wasn't helpful. I couldn't control the dot-com crash or the tremendous impact of 9/11 on the economy. I couldn't force an answer to why things had unfolded the way they did, nor could I predict what would come next. All I could do was show up each day, persist against the odds, and trust that the dots would eventually connect.

For eighteen months, I scoured job boards, applied endlessly, and endured interviews that often ended with rejection. The weight of uncertainty led to sleepless nights, anxiety, and dark days when doubt crept in. Was I compounding the situation with a bad decision? Would I ever find the next opportunity? But during that time, I also discovered something important: negative capability doesn't mean passive resignation. It means staying in the moment and maintaining faith, even when no clear answers exist.

I found inspiration from Alfred Lansing's *Endurance: Shackleton's Incredible Voyage*, which tells the story of Shackleton's crew surviving unimaginable hardship. While being unemployed for eighteen months wasn't the same as being stranded in Antarctica, I drew motivation from their survival and saw a parallel between his crew stuck on an iceberg and my frozen career.

Then, one day, fate, destiny, or luck intervened and offered me a job. Except this job was in Las Vegas at a relatively unknown advertising agency. They were about to launch a new tourism campaign and wanted me to help with media planning and buying. It wasn't the glamorous media role I had envisioned, and Las Vegas wasn't part of the plan, but I had learned to embrace uncertainty, so I said yes. That job turned out to be one of the defining moments in my career. The campaign we launched became "What Happens in Vegas Stays in Vegas," a globally recognized success. I went from watching the Super Bowl on my couch in January 2002 to attending it in person a year later.

In those eighteen months, I learned that the path to reconstruction isn't linear. It rarely makes sense at the moment and demands patience, persistence, and willingness to sit with the unknown. By embracing negative capability, I didn't let ambiguity paralyze me. Instead, I stayed open to possibility—and when the opportunity arrived, I was ready. Looking back, I can see that those eighteen months didn't define me as a failure. What defined me was my ability to endure, adapt, and eventually transform uncertainty into one of the greatest successes of my career.

How To: Ask Better Questions

You've navigated through the uncertainty of the last several weeks or months and are now rebuilding a path forward. Soon, there will be active job searches, interviews, and an assessment of what you want and how you'll get it. As you move through this phase, asking thoughtful, purposeful questions will be key to clarifying your goals and guiding your decisions. A crucial aspect will be the questions you ask and the mindful approach you take in asking them. By practicing the techniques outlined below, you can enhance your ability to elicit rich, informative responses that get to the heart of what you want to know.

1. Lead with intention. In essence, intention shapes the quality and purpose of your questions. When you're clear about what your desired outcome, it influences how you ask and how others respond. Before you engage in a meaningful conversation, take a moment to clarify your objectives. What do you hope to get out of this? What are the motivations guiding your words?

2. Consider the audience. Tailor your questions to the person you're speaking with, taking into account their background, knowledge, and perspective. This ensures your questions are relevant and respectful, making the conversation more engaging and productive. Pay attention to factors like age,

professional experience, and approach to communication, as these can significantly impact how they interpret and respond.

3. Ask follow-up questions. Don't hesitate to ask for clarification or request more details based on the responses you receive. This shows that you're engaged and genuinely interested, deepening the conversation. Follow-up questions allow for a more comprehensive understanding, which helps you make more informed decisions, while also making the other person feel heard and valued.

4. Be curious, not judgmental. Cultivate genuine curiosity rather than looking for confirmation of your beliefs or attempting to prove something. This open-minded approach will create a more honest and thoughtful dialogue. The people you interact with can sense your openness, authenticity, and eagerness to learn. When you approach conversations with curiosity, you create a safe space for deeper connections and mutual respect.

Asking better questions is a powerful skill that can transform every area of your life, from relationships to personal growth to decision-making. By adopting a growth mindset driven by curiosity, you improve your ability to connect with others, navigate challenges, and uncover meaningful insights.

When facing personal challenges, asking thoughtful, introspective questions can help clarify your priorities and guide you toward solutions. In everyday situations, engaging in intentional questioning can help you make wiser, more informed choices, whether related to finances, health, or long-term goals. In the context of networking or job interviews, asking insightful questions can set you apart, demonstrate your value, and provide deeper insights into the role and organization. Ultimately, practicing meaningful questioning enriches conversations, leading to a more purposeful, enriched life.

Roadmap Exercise: Habits and Routines

Even if you don't miss the early morning alarm telling you to get up and go to work, you may miss the structure it brought. I know I did. At first, being the master of my 9-to-5 schedule felt incredibly convenient, but over time, it became pretty horrible. I felt unstable without specific commitments to guide my time, without clear transitions marking my shifts in role or task, and without certain monotonous obligations that gave me a sense of productivity. I realized I needed to establish a new structure to bring stability and purpose to my day.

What do your days look like now? Do they feel blurry or in focus? Take some time to reflect on your daily rhythms, habits, and routines. In the lines below, write down what kind of structure you currently have in place. This can be as specific as setting an alarm clock or as vague as eating regular meals.

_____

_____

_____

_____

_____

_____

Look back at the professional goals you outlined in Chapter Three and the pursuit of joy you explored in Chapter Four. Are the daily habits and routines you've written down aligned with achieving those aspirations? Are they filling your cup? What new habits or routines can you create to facilitate growth during this transitional period? This could be professional (like dedicating time to network or updating your resume), personal (such as focusing on physical health or hobbies), or something in between (like improving skills for the sake of discovery).

_____

_____

_____

_____

_____

_____

Reframe: Embrace the Uncertainties Ahead as a Call for Reinvention

When faced with the unknown, we are often compelled to reevaluate our current paths, forcing us to shed outdated habits and mindsets. This process can spark creativity and inspire us to explore new avenues that align more closely with our evolving goals and desires. By accepting that change is a natural part of life, we can harness the energy of the unknown to reinvent ourselves, paving the way for exciting new possibilities and a more enriched future.

Stage Seven: Renewal

Renewal is when the path forward is revealed. Like the ebb and flow of the ocean, the tide of grief has receded to reveal a new horizon. The storm has passed, and there is an undeniable pull to move forward. But renewal isn't about picking up where you left off—it's about stepping into something new. It's about daring to dream again, rebuilding your career, and rediscovering your sense of purpose and direction. This experience, and the accompanying grief, has reshaped who you are, and now the question becomes: What will you do with this new version of yourself?

Don't think of this simply as recovery; it's a reinvention. Renewal is the audacity to believe in what comes next. President Obama famously spoke about "The Audacity of Hope" at the 2006 Democratic National Convention and in his memoir. In essence, it's the power of hope to drive change, even in the face of adversity. While Obama didn't frame the audacity of hope in the context of navigating a layoff, the concept certainly applies here.

It takes courage to navigate these stages of grief, and it requires hope that tomorrow will be better than today. It takes belief that your best days are ahead—that the resume will lead to an interview, and the interview will lead to a new job. Courage is what pushes you to keep applying after receiving rejection emails or being ghosted altogether. It's the strength to confront the discomfort, vulnerability, and self-doubt from repeated setbacks. Courage compels you to keep refining your resume and putting yourself out there, even when the outcome is unpredictable. It's about standing up after you've been knocked down.

Hope forces optimism when every ounce of your being wants to be pessimistic. Hope allows you to imagine a future where the personal growth found from this journey will be worth it, where you'll emerge stronger. It sparks willpower, which fuels perseverance. Hope is an emotional anchor that keeps the despair of rejection at bay and reminds you that each "no" brings you closer to the eventual "yes." Hope is a powerful motivator that allows us to step into the unknown, tackle new challenges, and grow from the experience.

When faced with 100 rejections, courage makes you send out the 101st job application. But it's hope that convinces you it's worth doing because the effort might finally pay off.

In this context, the audacity of hope allows us to take action despite fear. It also means being patient with yourself, understanding that hope doesn't necessarily manifest in instant success. It believes that small steps forward will eventually lead to something bigger and better.

Renewal is also a time to acknowledge how difficult this journey has been and celebrate your progress. While it has been painful, with each stage, you've taken steps toward healing, reassessing, and rebuilding. Renewal is when this growth is integrated into your being and becomes part of your life experience. But this change doesn't happen overnight. Much like nature's seasons, it's a gradual process that begins with small, meaningful changes. The lessons you've gathered, the strengths you've built, and the self-understanding you've cultivated are all part of this foundation. Allow yourself the grace to take this step at your own pace; renewal doesn't mean dismissing what you've lost but choosing to grow in new directions because of it. This stage offers you the chance to set intentions that align with your values, building a career—and a life—that is both fulfilling and resilient.

Embrace this time as an opportunity to intentionally shape what comes next. Even if it feels like stepping onto uncertain ground, know you are stepping forward with courage and a clearer sense of purpose. Let renewal remind you that while setbacks are inevitable, so is the possibility of starting anew—stronger, wiser, and hopeful for the future you're building.

Renewal is not only a philosophical concept; it often takes shape in the small, unexpected moments of our daily lives. It can be sparked by something as simple as a scent or sound, stirring powerful memories that bring clarity and closure. These moments remind us that healing and growth don't happen in a straight line but in waves, revealing their impact when we least expect it.

For example, I'll never forget how the smell of popcorn in a new workplace transported me back to a pivotal time in my career. If you like snacks, consider working at an advertising agency. Every agency I worked at always had a great snack closet. While the days may be long and the pay low, you could always be assured easy access to an assortment of sweet and salty snack options. Take your pick from chips, cereal, candy, cookies, granola bars, and popcorn—just to name a few.

The last agency I worked at in San Francisco proudly held a famous pink-and-white cookie company as a client, meaning the office was stocked with a wide assortment of cookies at all times. Because our brain processes smell in a way that ties it directly to emotions and memories, smell is often considered the most powerful of our senses. For instance, the smell of fresh-baked cookies might instantly remind you of your mother's kitchen as a child. Alas, the name Mother's Cookies was also the cookie company our agency represented.

After navigating the layoff from that agency, in the Fall of 2002, I found myself unexpectedly but gratefully working in Las Vegas on the new tourism campaign with the memorable catchphrase. One late afternoon, in my early days at this new job, I smelled popcorn popping in a nearby microwave. Fireworks of BOOM and POP traveled from my nose to my brain, and instantly, I was back at that agency in San Francisco. Closing my eyes, I could see, feel, hear, and smell the office and the people I had grown close to. A vivid wave of emotional explosions washed over me. The smell triggered a PTSD flashback that caused a total breakdown. Previously unprocessed emotions and grief came pouring out of me and I broke down and ugly cried.

That evening, a lot of things came into focus. It was a relief that the journey was finally over, and I was grateful for having crossed the divide. I felt pride in my courage and appreciation for the lessons learned. Ultimately, I felt a renewal. I recognized this was the beginning of a new chapter. It was the first day of the rest of my life.

The Cyclical Nature of New Beginnings

Mother Nature (not to be confused with Mother's Cookies) understands that loss is not an end but part of the larger cycle of life. In nature, impermanence, change, and creation are constant. Think about the seasonal shifts—from winter's stillness to spring's rebirth. The dark, cold months set the stage for new growth, showing us that beginnings often follow periods of dormancy or change. The same concept applies when facing something as personal as a job loss. While it may feel like the end of a chapter, it is also an opening for something new to take root. Ecosystems of all types and sizes remind us that the cycle of change, though uncomfortable, is necessary for new opportunities to flourish.

During this stage of grieving, renewal doesn't appear out of thin air—just like nature, it unfolds steadily, built on small, intentional steps forward. It becomes an invitation to recalibrate after working through the initial grief and gradually arriving at a sense of acceptance. It's a chance to assess the lessons learned, realign purpose with intent, and create space for a new beginning. This rebirth is about optimism and finding value in what comes next, whether it's pursuing a new career path, discovering hidden strengths, exploring passions once set aside, or building a lifestyle more aligned with personal values.

Consider the forest after a wildfire. At first, it looks devastated, stripped of life, and covered in ash—much like the aftermath of a job loss, where everything familiar seems destroyed and uncertain. But beneath the surface, seeds that require intense heat to sprout are now ready to germinate. Within months, new growth begins, and over time, the forest renews itself—often more diverse and resilient than before. This cycle shows us that what appears to be destruction is often part of nature's process of creating new life. It serves as a powerful reminder that renewal is not just possible but inevitable with time and effort. With effort, loss can clear space for something unexpected and valuable to take root.

Turtles, particularly the honu (green sea turtle), hold deep spiritual and cultural significance in Hawaiian culture. The honu is a symbol of longevity, endurance, and wisdom. It represents a connection to the ocean, the land, and the ancestors. It is revered for its ability to navigate vast distances, embodying the journey of life and the resilience required to face challenges.

The analogy of a turtle outgrowing its shell may feel particularly fitting for this stage of personal growth and transformation. As the turtle matures, it needs a larger shell to accommodate its expanding body. If the turtle doesn't adapt to a new shell, it will become restricted and unable to continue growing.

Similarly, you may feel you've outgrown your old role, identity, or life structure after this experience. The shell you've been living in—the job and the comfort it provided—may no longer fit. In the renewal process, just as a turtle must adapt its shell, you may need to shed the identity you once held to create room for a new self. This might mean reimagining your identity, exploring new interests, or pursuing different opportunities.

Life, much like the changing seasons or the turtle's shell, is always in a state of renewal. Evoking the song lyrics from "Closing Time" by Semisonic: "Every new beginning comes from some other beginning's end."

An Extraordinary Comeback

In 1985, Steve Jobs was ousted from Apple, the company he co-founded and poured his heart and vision into, in a dramatic and highly publicized boardroom battle. His dismissal was not just a professional blow; it struck at the core of his identity. Jobs later described the experience as one of the most painful periods of his life, leaving him in a state of shock and disbelief. It was a time of self-reflection, forcing him to confront feelings of inadequacy and failure. It was a turning point that, while devastating at the moment, ultimately became a catalyst for profound personal and professional transformation.

Initially, Jobs struggled with denial, grappling with the reality of being let go from the company he had built. He fluctuated between anger at those he felt had betrayed him and refusing to accept the board's decision. He lashed out publicly and privately toward those he perceived as enemies, including former colleagues. This anger fueled his determination to prove his worth and regain his footing in the tech industry.

The bargaining phase manifested in Jobs' next venture, aptly named NeXT, a company he founded to develop technology that could rival or surpass Apple's achievements. Through NeXT, Jobs sought to prove that his vision and innovation could thrive independently, using the venture to regain his confidence and reshape his legacy after his ousting. However, NeXT faced financial and operational struggles, and Jobs descended into a period of depression, questioning his abilities and the future of his career.

Acceptance gradually began to take hold as Jobs redirected his focus and energy toward new opportunities. During this time, he acquired Pixar, a small animation studio that would redefine and ultimately revolutionize the film industry. Jobs immersed himself in this venture, leveraging his visionary instincts to transform Pixar into a powerhouse, releasing iconic films like *Toy Story*. This chapter marked a significant shift: rather than dwelling on his ousting from Apple, Jobs focused on restructuring his career, channeling his creativity and ambition into ventures aligned with his passions. His time away from Apple allowed him to mature as a leader, cultivating a deeper understanding of teamwork, innovation, and humility.

Jobs' ultimate renewal came full circle in 1997 when Apple, struggling to stay afloat, acquired NeXT, bringing him back into the fold. This time, he returned not as the brash young visionary but as a more seasoned and intentional leader, ready to guide Apple in a bold new direction. Under his leadership, the company recovered and revolutionized the tech industry with groundbreaking products like the iPod, iPhone, and iPad. Jobs' journey—from dismissed founder to the leader who saved Apple—is a testament to the emotional complexities of job loss and the transformative power of resilience, self-reflection, and reinvention. His ability to navigate the stages of grief and emerge stronger is an inspiring example of how setbacks can ultimately lead to extraordinary comebacks.

The Role of Intentions in Career Development

There are a lot of exciting, vulnerable, and pivotal career decisions coming your way. Many factors will shape your choices, but approaching them on solid footing—meaning you're clear on the *why* behind your actions—will anchor you when the doubt creeps in, when the distractions pull you away, and when the easy path tempts you.

A study called *The Role of Intentions in Career Development*, published in the *Counseling Psychology Commons*, reveals a powerful truth: our conscious and subconscious intentions profoundly impact our career paths, especially after life-altering events like job loss. In the final stage of grief following a layoff, embracing the power of intention becomes a turning point—a shift from simply surviving to actively designing your future. At this stage, you're not just processing the past; you're making deliberate choices about where you want to go next and how you want to grow.

Career development isn't just about polishing your resume or chasing the next opportunity. It's about setting meaningful, intentional goals. During renewal, when emotions may still be raw, focusing on intention offers clarity and hope. Research shows that setting strong, positive intentions—such as pursuing work aligned with your values or exploring new possibilities—leads to greater professional success and personal fulfillment. This intentionality restores a sense of control, transforming the upheaval of a layoff into a launchpad for growth and purpose.

The study also emphasizes the power of self-reflection in this journey. After a layoff, you have a unique opportunity to pause and ask yourself what you want to do and why. This introspection can be transformative, aligning your career decisions with your deeper values. While it may not feel like it at first, this can become one of the most enriching periods in your career—where intention-driven choices create a path that feels authentic and deeply rewarding.

The renewal stage is about channeling the emotions of grief into a sense of purpose, crafting a career that resonates with who you are and what you aspire to achieve. This is your opportunity to turn a setback into a comeback, one intentional step at a time.

This idea of finding your "why" echoes Simon Sinek's concept of "Start with Why," which argues that successful individuals and organizations understand and can articulate their core purpose or "why." In his book *Start with Why: How Great Leaders Inspire Everyone to Take Action*, Sinek highlights Steve Jobs' "why" and its manifestation into the ethos of Apple as a significant factor in the company's success. When Jobs returned to Apple in 1997, his goal wasn't just to build great products; it was to change how people interacted with technology—making it more accessible, intuitive, and beautiful. This vision (or "why") drove Apple's product development, marketing, and growth. It challenged the status quo and sought to empower everyone with user-friendly and elegantly crafted products.

While Apple has a legacy of rebelling against conformity (google the 1984 Super Bowl ad to see one of the most iconic and celebrated commercials of all time), Jobs' vision took it even further. He encouraged employees and consumers to "Think Different" about technology and subsequently created products that forever changed their role in our lives. "Think Different" became another iconic ad campaign, positioning the company as a visionary leader. It was designed to appeal to those who saw technology as a tool to change the world, not just convenience. Regardless of how one views the impact of these changes, Jobs' legacy underscores the power of intentionality: with a clear "why" guiding your choices, you can transform setbacks into opportunities, creating work that not only fulfills you but also has the potential to reshape the world around you.

How To: Lead With Intention

Reentering the workforce after a layoff can feel like stepping into uncharted waters. But leading with intention transforms this challenge into an opportunity for growth and reinvention, allowing you to recalibrate and redefine your career on your terms. When you're intentional about what you're seeking, you stop chasing every opportunity and pursue the ones that truly fit.

I wish I could say I was intentional about every job I've applied for or accepted. Unfortunately, that's far from the truth. Like many, I've started job hunts hopeful and optimistic about what lay ahead. However, after eighteen months of unemployment, any job starts to look good, even if it's located in Las Vegas. I understand the urgency—when unemployment benefits, work visas, or health insurance run out, the pressure to find work can feel unbearable.

The odds of reemployment after a layoff are heavily stacked against applicants (not similar to Las Vegas betting odds being stacked against the player). On average, you might receive one or two job offers for every hundred resumes sent out. And let's be honest: most of those offers won't resemble your dream job. Balancing a job that pays the bills with one that fulfills your purpose is rarely straightforward.

For some, fulfillment may come from stepping off the traditional path entirely—perhaps venturing out independently and charting a course via entrepreneurship. That said, you can nurture your dream job while still punching the clock at the widget factory.

On a micro level, my pivots more closely resemble the turning oil tanker than they do anything else. But when I zoom out and examine the arc of my career, I see how each subtle pivot altered the trajectory of my path. It's a journey that spans advertising, marketing, and sales across industries like technology, tourism, hospitality, and retail. A path that began in advertising agencies, evolved into client-side marketing, transitioned into independent consulting, and now includes work as an independent author.

I didn't discover this road after my first layoff, and you may not either—and that's okay. Everyone's journey is unique; there is no right or wrong path to discovery.

As you submit job applications, zero in on the opportunities that excite you, challenge you, and align with your values. It may only be one out of every ten (or fewer), but they're the ones deserving of your time and energy. When engaging with potential employers, frame your time away as a deliberate period of reflection and growth. Emphasize how it has prepared you to bring fresh perspectives and renewed energy to your next role. This approach demonstrates that you're not merely seeking a job but charting a purposeful path forward.

Another essential aspect of leading with intention is managing how you show up during your job search. Networking becomes less about asking for help and more about building genuine, mutually beneficial connections. Engage thoughtfully with your network, whether it's through LinkedIn, professional groups, or industry events. Share your story with confidence and authenticity, focusing on your future goals rather than just the past. People respond to clarity and purpose; your intentionality will stand out as you build relationships and discover opportunities.

Finally, be deliberate about your next step. Intentionality doesn't mean perfection; it means making decisions that serve your goals, whatever they may be. Circumstances may dictate immediacy and a means to pay bills. But don't let short-term goals derail your long-term vision. By leading with intention, you'll not only find your next role—you'll also lay the groundwork for a career that's meaningful, fulfilling, and uniquely yours.

Roadmap Exercise: Finding Your Why

We've concluded each chapter with exercises designed to help you navigate the emotional and practical challenges of job loss while setting a strong foundation for the future. The first exercise focused on finances, encouraging you to assess your financial situation honestly and create a realistic budget. By gaining clarity on your financial footing, you reduced anxiety and made informed decisions during this transitional period. The second chapter dove into guiding principles, asking you to identify your core values and beliefs. That reflective process provided a compass for decision-making and ensured alignment between your next steps and what truly matters to you.

As your journey progressed, you explored professional goals and the pursuit of joy. The exercises prompted you to define your career aspirations while considering how you want to feel and grow in your next role. Additionally, focusing on joy encourages you to reconnect with activities and experiences that fulfill you, reinforcing the importance of finding balance and meaning beyond work. Those exercises around strengths and weaknesses helped you gain self-awareness, allowing you to leverage your skills and address areas for growth. That stage was pivotal in building confidence and shaping a compelling narrative for future opportunities.

Finally, habits and routines emerged, emphasizing the importance of structure during uncertain times. You were guided to evaluate those daily habits, letting go of those that no longer serve you and introducing routines that foster resilience and productivity. Each chapter's exercises collectively served as a roadmap, guiding you through grief and uncertainty toward a renewed sense of purpose and empowerment. By actively engaging with these tools, you have emerged stronger, more intentional, and ready to embrace the next chapter of your professional journey.

As you move into this next chapter of your journey, discovering your "why" becomes your most powerful tool. This isn't just about identifying the right job—it's about understanding what drives you and curating a life that reflects your core values and aspirations. Renewal is your opportunity to reset and approach the future with purpose and meaning. But how do you ensure your next steps align with what truly matters to you?

In this final exercise, you'll define what discovering your "why" means for you. Reflect on the insights you've gained throughout this process. What motivates you at a deeper level? What specific impact do you aspire to make in your next role? How does this next chapter connect with your broader vision for your career and life? Beyond salary or title, how will you measure success in a way that resonates with your sense of purpose?

Think of this as your personal roadmap—a guide to uncovering and living your "why." Use the space below to articulate your motivations and vision. This exercise isn't just about securing your next role; it's about crafting a life that feels meaningful, aligned, and authentically yours.

_____

_____

_____

_____

_____

_____

Reframe: The End Is Just the Beginning

After a layoff, the final stages of grief often bring clarity and a new sense of direction. The end of this chapter—and subsequently, this book—signals the beginning of another. But this time, you're the author. This is your chance to reassess your next steps, redefine your goals, and apply what you've learned to write a new beginning. The skills and experiences you've gained remain invaluable, ready to serve as tools for what comes next. I hope that what felt like an ending becomes an opportunity to begin again, with a newfound purpose and strength.

Author's Note

Thank you for joining me as I shared my layoff journey—the messy emotions, the valuable lessons, and the growth that came with it. You've already taken courageous steps on your own path through job loss, and there is so much more for you to uncover. I hope the insights and strategies shared here have resonated with you and provided a meaningful roadmap for navigating this challenging chapter.

I'd love to hear your story too—how you're processing this experience and moving forward. Visit www.TheSteveJaffe.com to share your journey. Let's connect, support one another, and transform these setbacks into stepping stones for a brighter future. Remember, your journey doesn't end here; it's just the beginning of your transformation.

Acknowledgments

Throughout my life, friends and family have often encouraged me to write a book. Truthfully, it's something I've always wanted to do, but I never felt I had a compelling enough subject matter to dedicate myself to the endeavor—until the summer of 2023, when I was laid off for the fourth and final time. This reduction in force impacted approximately 20% of the company, including close colleagues and team members. Some were just beginning their careers, while others were facing their second layoff in less than a year. I wanted to communicate the lessons I had learned during my own layoff journey. I wanted to help them, tell them I understood, and offer guidance. This has been my North Star and the inspiration behind sharing my story.

Writing this book has been as transformative as the journey it describes. Thank you to my family and friends, who offered their steadfast support and encouragement, believing in me even when my confidence faltered. To my mentors and colleagues, who generously shared their wisdom and experiences: your insights formed the backbone of this book. I am forever grateful to each of you for helping me bring this story to life.

This book would not exist without the unshakable support, encouragement, and love of my wife, Amoreena. She has inspired my recovery and helped me navigate my reinvention. She believed in me on those nights when I had nothing but doubt. Her unwavering belief in my potential became the foundation upon which this journey was built, and for that, I am forever grateful.

Special thanks to Jane Jaffe, Larry Jaffe, Lisa Jaffe, Grace Jaffe, Dylan Jaffe, Jean Schiavo, Jehr Schiavo, Ann Foster, Jackie Davis, Val Hardie, Rachael Brown, Don James, Kimberly Hutchins, Matt Morgan, Keith Newton, Darrel Redford, Daren Lipinsky, Kristin Thompson, Krista Morgan, and Patricia Folgar.

Thank you to every person holding this book who has faced the uncertainty and heartache of a layoff—your resilience inspired these pages. I hope this book becomes a companion and a source of strength for your own journey to discovery.

Endnotes

Introduction

"For perspective, according to McMaster University sociology professor Art Budros": Budros, A. (2004). Rationality, the adoption of downsizing, and institutionalism. *Social Forces, 76*(1), 229-250.

"A McKinsey survey of 2,000 U.S. companies": McKinsey & Company. (2009). *Managing in the downturn: Short-term survival and long-term growth.* McKinsey & Company. Retrieved 2024 from https://www.mckinsey.com

"In 2022, 17.6 million Americans were laid off": Bureau of Labor Statistics. *Monthly Labor Review.* U.S. Department of Labor, 2022, 72.3 million separations, inclusive page numbers not available.

"40% of Americans have been laid off at least once in their career": The Harris Poll. (2019). *U.S. Layoff Anxiety and Preparedness Survey Report.* INTOO. Retrieved 2024 from https://www.intoo.com

Stage One: Denial

"About 75% of US employees are 'at-will,'": HCAMag. (n.d.). *At-will employment: Everything you need to know.* Retrieved 2024 from https://www.hcamag.com/us/specialization/employment-law/at-will-employment-everything-you-need-to-know/318985

"In case you're not familiar with WorldCom": Investopedia. (n.d.). *The WorldCom scandal: A timeline.* Retrieved 2024 from https://www.investopedia.com/articles/07/011607.asp; Corporate Finance Institute. (n.d.). *WorldCom: A case study in corporate fraud.* Retrieved 2024 from https://corporatefinanceinstitute.com/resources/knowledge/finance/worldcom-case-study

The Grace in Denial: Lo, B., & Glickman, S. (2018). *The ethics of "ethical" challenges in healthcare: A new vision for the future. New England Journal of Medicine,* 379(11), 1085-1090. https://doi.org/10.1056/NEJMp1810685

The Myth of Meritocracy: Sandel, M. J. (2018, October 19). The myth of meritocracy: Who really gets what they deserve. *The Guardian.* Retrieved 2024 from https://www.theguardian.com/news/2018/oct/19/the-myth-of-meritocracy-who-really-gets-what-they-deserve; Hope, K. (1985). IQ + effort = merit. In *As Others See Us: Schooling and Social Mobility in Scotland and the United States* (pp. 63–75). chapter, Cambridge: Cambridge University Press.

"Since Elon Musk took over the company in October 2022"; "Some were notified via an email"; "...their badges were deactivated": The Cartwright Law Firm, Inc. (2022). *Twitter layoffs and legal claims: An overview.* Retrieved 2024 from https://www.cartwrightlawfirm.com

"As a result, Musk has faced multiple class action lawsuits": Alvarez, S. (2024, July 10). Elon Musk and X beat $500M severance pay lawsuit from ex-Twitter staff. *Teslarati*. Retrieved 2024 from https://www.teslarati.com

"One employee who was already in the building": Glynn, K. (2022, November 4). *"Are you saying no to Elon Musk?": Scenes from the slash-and-burn buyout of Twitter.* Vanity Fair. Retrieved 2024 from https://www.vanityfair.com/news/story/elon-musk-twitter-buyout

"Similar scenarios would be repeated at another Musk company": The Guardian. (2024, April 15). *Tesla to cut 14,000 jobs as Elon Musk seeks to reduce costs.* Retrieved 2024 from https://www.theguardian.com/technology/2024/apr/15/tesla-cut-jobs-elon-musk-staff

"Esther Crawford, a Chief Executive of Payments at Twitter": Pearson, J. (2023, February 27). Twitter lays off manager who slept on office floor after Musk takeover. *Vice*. Retrieved 2024 from https://www.vice.com; Schiffer, Z. (2022, November 2). Esther Crawford, who went viral for sleeping on the floor at Twitter, was laid off. *Platformer*. Retrieved 2024 from https://www.platformer.news

"Then there is the story of Nico Murillo": Business Today. (2024, May 1). *'Showered at factory, slept in parking lot': A Tesla employee's layoff story goes viral.* Business Today. Retrieved 2024 from https://www.businesstoday.in; Moyer, L. (2024, April 30). *Tesla employee's viral LinkedIn post about sacrifices and layoff sparks debate.* Platformer. Retrieved 2024 from https://www.platformer.news

How To: Process Emotions in Healthy Ways: Keller, S. (2023, January 4). *Managing your emotions after being laid off.* Harvard Business Review. https://hbr.org/2023/01/managing-your-emotions-after-being-laid-off

Stage Two: Pain

The Psychology of Pain: Osterweis, M., Kleinman, A., & Mechanic, D. (Eds.). (1987). *Pain and disability: Clinical, behavioral, and public policy perspectives* (Chapter 7: The anatomy and physiology of pain). National Academies Press. https://doi.org/10.17226/993;
Harvard Health Publishing. (n.d.). *Understanding the stress response.* Harvard Health. Retrieved 2024 from https://www.health.harvard.edu/staying-healthy/understanding-the-stress-response;
Kiecolt-Glaser, J. K., McGuire, L., Robles, T. F., & Glaser, R. (2010). Psychoneuroimmunology: Psychological influences on immune function and health. *Proceedings of the National Academy of Sciences, 107*(15), 69–74. https://doi.org/10.1073/pnas.1102693108

"When physical pain is unrelieved, it triggers a stress response in the body": Fisher, N. (2020, February 14). Emotional & physical pain are almost the same to your brain. *Forbes.* https://www.forbes.com/sites/nicolefisher/2020/02/14/emotional--physical-pain-are-almost-the-sameto-your-brain/

"Layoffs have been linked to an increase in divorce, depression, and cardiovascular disease": Akilléwald, F. (n.d.). *Money, work, and marital stability.* Harvard University.

Retrieved 2024 from
https://scholar.harvard.edu/files/akillewald/files/money_work
_and_marital_stability.pdf;

Guerra, O.; Eboreime, E. The Impact of Economic Recessions on Depression, Anxiety, and Trauma-Related Disorders and Illness Outcomes—A Scoping Review. *Behav. Sci.* 2021, 11, 119. https://doi.org/10.3390/bs11090119;

Albertsen, K., Damsgaard, M. T., & Benn, M. (2022). The impact of job loss on cardiovascular health: A systematic review and meta-analysis. *European Heart Journal, 43*(8), 716-728. https://doi.org/10.1093/eurheartj/ehac029

"...chronic stress of unemployment, financial insecurity, and loss of health insurance": Liu, X., Hoven, C. W., & Cohen, P. (2013). *Mental health consequences of job loss: A review of the literature. PMC* (PubMed Central).

https://pmc.ncbi.nlm.nih.gov/articles/PMC3855327/

"...such as obesity, diabetes, and alcohol-related disorders": Feigl AB, Goryakin Y, Devaux M, Lerouge A, Vuik S, Cecchini M. *The short-term effect of BMI, alcohol use, and related chronic conditions on labor market outcomes: A time-lag panel analysis utilizing European SHARE dataset.* PLoS One. 2019 Mar 11;14(3):e0211940. doi: 10.1371/journal.pone.0211940. PMID: 30856184; PMCID: PMC6411140;

He, J., Zhang, M., Liu, Y., & Li, J. (2023). *Impact of long-term unemployment on obesity and metabolic health: A systematic review and meta-analysis.* The American Journal of Clinical Nutrition. https://ajcn.nutrition.org/article/S0002-9165(23)66352-X/fulltext

"If Mark Zuckerberg had known about these effects":
Zuckerberg, M. (2022, November 9). *Mark Zuckerberg's message to employees on layoffs.* Meta. Retrieved 2024 from
https://about.fb.com/news/2022/11/mark-zuckerberg-layoff-message-to-employees;
Bercovici, J. (2023, March 14). *Meta to lay off 10,000 employees as part of "year of efficiency".* Business Insider. Retrieved 2024 from
https://www.businessinsider.com/meta-layoffs?utm_source=chatgpt.com

Survivor guilt: HRD Connect. (2024, June 18). *The other side of layoffs: Survivor guilt.* HRD Connect.
https://www.hrdconnect.com/2024/06/18/the-other-side-of-layoffs-survivor-guilt/;
CBS News. (2023, November 11). *Layoff survivor guilt: How tech layoffs are affecting the employees who remain.* CBS News.
https://www.cbsnews.com/news/layoff-survivor-guilt-tech-layoffs/

"It's been estimated that the percentage of jobs": The Institution of Engineering and Technology. (n.d.). *The hidden job market.* The Institution of Engineering and Technology.
https://www.theiet.org/career-and-learning/career-support/finding-a-job/hidden-job-market/;
HRD Connect. (2024, June 18). *The other side of layoffs: Survivor guilt.* HRD Connect.
https://www.hrdconnect.com/2024/06/18/the-other-side-of-layoffs-survivor-guilt/

"Aerobic exercise, in particular, has been shown": McIntyre KM, Puterman E, Scodes JM, et al.

The effects of aerobic training on subclinical negative affect: A randomized controlled trial. *Health Psychol.* 2020;39(4):255-264. doi:10.1037/hea0000836

Stage Three: Negotiation

"Meta Founder, Chairman, and CEO Mark Zuckerberg recently stated": Fast Company. (2024, October 17). Mark Zuckerberg's 'year of efficiency' is turning into a multiyear effort as Meta gets hit with another round of layoffs. *Fast Company.* https://www.fastcompany.com/mark-zuckerbergs-year-of-efficiency-meta-gets-hit-with-layoffs; Zuckerberg, M. (2022, November 9). Mark Zuckerberg's message to Meta employees. *Meta.* https://about.fb.com/news/2022/11/layoffs-2022

"...Older Workers Benefit Protection Act passed into law by Congress in 1990": U.S. Equal Employment Opportunity Commission. (n.d.). *Q&A-Understanding waivers of discrimination claims in employee severance agreements.* U.S. Equal Employment Opportunity Commission. Retrieved 2024 from https://www.eeoc.gov

"As of April 23, 2024, the US Federal Trade Commission voted": Federal Trade Commission. (2024, April 23). *FTC issues final rule banning most noncompete clauses in employer agreements.* https://www.ftc.gov/news-events/press-releases/2024/04/ftc-issues-final-rule-banning-most-noncompete-clauses-employer-agreements

"In 2013, Walt Disney Company announced": Program on Negotiation at Harvard Law School. (2012, December 18).

Famous negotiators feature in top negotiations of 2012. Harvard Law School. https://www.pon.harvard.edu/daily/negotiation-skills-daily/famous-negotiators-feature-in-top-negotiations-of-2012/

"In early 2021, pharmaceutical company Merck": Goldstein, D. (2021, February 10). Merck halts development of its Covid vaccine. *The New York Times*. https://www.nytimes.com/2021/02/10/health/merck-covid-vaccine.html;
Rovner, J. (2021, March 3). How the White House got 2 pharma foes to work together on COVID-19 vaccine. *NPR*. https://www.npr.org/2021/03/03/973117712/how-the-white-house-got-2-pharma-foes-to-work-together-on-covid-19-vaccine

"Also in 2021, Swiss pharmaceutical firm Novartis and French drugmaker": Reuters. (2021, January 29). Swiss drugmaker Novartis to help make Pfizer-BioNTech COVID-19 vaccine. *Reuters*. https://www.reuters.com/business/healthcare-pharmaceuticals/swiss-drugmaker-novartis-help-make-pfizer-biontech-covid-19-vaccine-2021-01-29/

"...Sanofi helped Pfizer and BioNTech produce their highly effective Covid-19 vaccine": Sanofi. (2021, January 27). *Sanofi to support Pfizer-BioNTech COVID-19 vaccine production*. Sanofi. https://www.sanofi.com/en/media-room/press-releases/2021/2021-01-27-06-30-00-2164797

"In 2022, the U.S. national women's soccer team celebrated an enormous win": Bai, M. (2022, February 22). U.S. women's soccer team reaches historic deal for equal pay. *The New York Times*.

https://www.nytimes.com/2022/02/22/sports/soccer/us-womens-soccer-equal-pay.html

"The cast of *Friends* famously went this route as well": Hoffman, J. (2016, October 19). How the 'Friends' cast got $1 million per episode salary. *Business Insider.* https://www.businessinsider.com/how-friends-cast-got-1-million-per-episode-salary-2016-10

"Sixteen years later, six cast members from the sitcom *Modern Family*": Reuters. (2012, May 1). *'Modern Family' stars sue over contracts. Reuters.* https://www.reuters.com/article/business/modern-family-stars-sue-over-contracts-idUSL4E8IO8A3/

The Inevitability of Option B: Sandberg, S., & Grant, A. (2017). *Option B: facing adversity, building resilience, and finding joy.* First large print edition. New York, Random House Large Print.

Stage Four: Depression

"A 2022 study on the link between depression and unemployment": McCarthy, J. (2014, July 15). *Depression rates higher among long-term unemployed.* Gallup. https://news.gallup.com/poll/171044/depression-rates-higher-among-long-term-unemployed.aspx

"A Rutgers University study on long-term unemployment": Heldrich Center for Workforce Development. (2011). *Out of work and losing hope: The misery and bleak expectations of American workers.* Edward J. Bloustein School of Planning and Public

Policy, Rutgers University. Available at
https://heldrich.rutgers.edu

"An immigrant woman was recently let go from X (formerly Twitter)": Tabahriti, S. (2022, November 4). A fired Twitter employee who's 6 months pregnant tells the company 'see you in court'. *Business Insider.*
https://www.businessinsider.nl/a-fired-twitter-employee-whos-6-month-pregnant-tells-the-company-see-you-in-court/

The Correlation Between Employment and Self-Esteem: Bernick, M. S. (1981). The Overlooked Relation between Self-Esteem and Work. *Political Psychology, 3*(3/4), 211–220.
https://doi.org/10.2307/3791149

"...83% of Americans believe having a good career is vital to their self-esteem": Skynova. (2022, August 5). *Work and self-worth: How your career impacts your self-esteem.*
https://www.skynova.com/blog/work-and-self-worth

"A major study by a social scientist at Yale": Bakke, E. W. (1940). *Citizens without work: A study of the effects of unemployment upon the workers' social relations and practices.* Yale University Press.

"Only about 25% of applicants who start Navy SEAL training": Navy SEALs. (n.d.). *Hell week: The toughest challenge in Navy SEAL training.* Navy SEALs.
https://navyseals.com/nsw/hell-week-0/

"Research has shown that candidates who experience their first-ever major setbacks": Military Mental Endurance. (n.d.). *Overcoming obstacles: 8 lessons in resilience from Navy SEALs.* Military

Mental Endurance.
https://militarymentalendurance.com/overcoming-obstacles-8-lessons-in-resilience-from-navy-seals;
Program on Negotiation at Harvard Law School. (n.d.).
Overcoming obstacles: Navy SEALs and mental toughness. Harvard
Law School. https://www.pon.harvard.edu/daily/negotiation-skills-daily

"The underlying pathophysiological basis of depression":
Cherry, K. (2023, June 15). *The chemistry of depression.* Verywell
Mind. https://www.verywellmind.com/the-chemistry-of-depression-1065137

"When we're exposed to severe and chronic stress":
Duman, R. S., & Aghajanian, G. K. (2012). Synaptic dysfunction
in depression: Potential therapeutic targets. *Science*, 338(6103),
68-72. https://doi.org/10.1126/science.1222938;
Krishnan, V., & Nestler, E. J. (2008). The molecular
neurobiology of depression. *Nature*, 455(7215), 894-902.
https://doi.org/10.1038/nature07455;
Frontiers in Neuroscience. (2016, May 25). Depression as a glial-based synaptic dysfunction. *Frontiers in Neuroscience.*
https://www.frontiersin.org/articles/10.3389/fnins.2016.00274/full

"Serotonin is essential for gut health": Sweeney, L. (2020,
May 19). *How serotonin affects the gut: A link between mood and
digestion.* Medical News Today.
https://www.medicalnewstoday.com/articles/324312;

Mian, M.A. (2020). Serotonin reuptake inhibitors and the gut microbiome: Significance of the gut microbiome in relation to mechanism of action, treatment response, side effects, and tachyphylaxis. *Frontiers in Neuroscience.* https://www.frontiersin.org/articles/10.3389/fnins.2020.00718/full

The Bright Side of Being Blue: Andrews P. W., Thomson J. A. Jr. The bright side of being blue: depression as an adaptation for analyzing complex problems. *Psychol Rev.* 2009 Jul;116(3):620-54. doi: 10.1037/a0016242. PMID: 19618990; PMCID: PMC2734449; https://pmc.ncbi.nlm.nih.gov/articles/PMC2734449/

"Research shows that everyday tasks like loading the dishwasher": Hanley, A. W., Warner, A. R., Dehili, V. M., Canto, A. I. Garland, E. L. *Washing Dishes to Wash the Dishes: Brief Instruction in an Informal Mindfulness Practice.* Mindfulness, 2014; 6 (5): 1095 DOI: 10.1007/s12671-014-0360-9

Stage Five: Acceptance

"In the early 1930s, an American theologian": Niebuhr, R. (1932). *The Serenity Prayer.*

Mindset Shift: Radical Acceptance: Smith, S. (2022, March 7). The healing power of radical acceptance. *Psychology Today.* https://www.psychologytoday.com/us/blog/being-your-best-self/202203/the-healing-power-of-radical-acceptance

"In the late 1980s and early 1990s, American psychologist Dr. Marsha Linehan": Linehan, M. (1993). *Cognitive-behavioral treatment of borderline personality disorder.* The Guilford Press.

Acceptance as a Regulation Strategy: Wojnarowska, A., Kobylinska, D., & Lewczuk, K. (2020). Acceptance as an emotion regulation strategy in experimental psychological research: What we know and how we can improve that knowledge. *Frontiers in Psychology, 11*, 242. https://doi.org/10.3389/fpsyg.2020.00242;
Hall, K. (n.d.). *Radical acceptance in DBT: For mental health healing.* Counseling Center Group. Retrieved 2024 from https://counselingcentergroup.com/radical-acceptance-therapy;
Peña-Vargas, C., Armaiz-Peña, G., & Castro-Figueroa, E. (2021). A biopsychosocial approach to grief, depression, and the role of emotional regulation. *Behavioral Sciences, 11*(8), 110. https://doi.org/10.3390/bs11080110;
Fernández-Alcántara, M., Kokou-Kpolou, C. K., Cruz-Quintana, F., & Pérez-Marfil, M. N. (2021). Editorial: New perspectives in bereavement and loss: Complicated and disenfranchised grief along the life cycle. *Frontiers in Psychology, 12*, 691464. https://doi.org/10.3389/fpsyg.2021.691464

The Art of Noble Lessons: Blakely, S. (2020). Sara Blakely: Start small, think big, scale fast. Cord Magazine. https://cordmagazine.com;
The Conferences for Women. (2025). Sara Blakely. National Conference for Women. https://www.nationalconferenceforwomen.org/speakers/sara-blakely/;
CheatSheet. (2023, May 17). *Guest Shark and Spanx founder Sara Blakely says this question helped her become a success.* CheatSheet.

https://www.cheatsheet.com/entertainment/guest-shark-and-spanx-founder-sara-blakely-says-this-question-helped-her-become-a-success.html/

"Gratitude doesn't always come naturally during difficult times": The Berkeley Well-Being Institute. (n.d.). *Gratitude: Definition, examples, & benefits.* Retrieved 2024 from https://www.berkeleywellbeing.com/gratitude

Stage Six: Reconstruction

The Ship of Theseus: Wasserman, R. (2021). Material constitution. In E. N. Zalta (Ed.), *The Stanford Encyclopedia of Philosophy* (Fall 2021 Edition). Stanford University. Retrieved 2024 from https://plato.stanford.edu/archives/fall2021/entries/material-constitution/

Rebounding Through Resilience: Pivot: The Only Move That Matters Is Your Next One: Blake, J. (2016). *Pivot: The only move that matters is your next one.* Portfolio/Penguin.

Vera Wang: Beard, A. (2019, July). Life's work: An interview with Vera Wang. *Harvard Business Review.* Retrieved 2024 from https://hbr.org/2019/07/lifes-work-an-interview-with-vera-wang;
CBS News. (2013, May 30). *Vera Wang talks bridal inspiration, how she applies fashion sense to wedding style.*
https://www.cbsnews.com/news/vera-wang-talks-bridal-inspiration-how-she-applies-fashion-sense-to-wedding-style/

Colonel Harland Sanders: Klein, C. (2015, September 9). *8 facts about the real Colonel Sanders and the founding of KFC. History.* Updated July 12, 2024. Retrieved 2024 from https://www.history.com/news/8-facts-real-colonel-sanders-kfc

Ina Garten: Garten, I. (n.d.). *About.* Barefoot Contessa. Retrieved 2024 from https://barefootcontessa.com/about

Jack Ma: Britannica. (n.d.). *Jack Ma.* In *Britannica Money.* Retrieved 2024 from https://www.britannica.com/money/Jack-Ma

Ray Kroc: FranchiseWire. (2021, April 15). *Ray Kroc and the McDonald's story.* Retrieved 2024 from https://www.franchisewire.com/ray-kroc-and-the-mcdonalds-story/

Oprah Winfrey: Vogue. (2017, January 5). *Oprah Winfrey: 5 things you didn't know.* Retrieved 2024 from https://www.vogue.com/article/oprah-winfrey-5-things-you-didnt-know

Steve Jobs: ABC News. (2011, October 6). *Steve Jobs on being fired from his own company.* Retrieved 2024 from https://abcnews.go.com/Technology/steve-jobs-fire-company/story?id=14683754

Walt Disney: Nesterova, O. (2023, January 5). *Walt Disney: Imagination has no age.* Medium. Retrieved 2024 from https://medium.com/@onestpreneur/walt-disney-imagination-has-no-age-dfb9a875598a

The great unknown/negative culpability: Poetry Foundation. (n.d.). *Negative capability.* Poetry Foundation. Retrieved 2024 from https://www.poetryfoundation.org/education/glossary/negative-capability;
Thinking Literature. (2021). *Keats and the concept of negative capability: A deeper exploration.* Thinking Literature. Retrieved 2024 from https://academic.oup.com/liverpool-scholarship-online/book/30851;
Keats, J. (1817, December 22). *Letter to George and Tom Keats.* In *Selections from Keats's Letters.* Poetry Foundation. Retrieved 2024 from https://www.poetryfoundation.org/articles/69384/selections-from-keatss-letters

"It's estimated that five million people nationwide lost their jobs": Wisniewski, T. (2021, December 1). *The dot-com bubble: The infamous economic meltdown.* Axiory Intelligence. Retrieved 2024 from https://axioryintelligence.com/education/infographics/the-dot-com-bubble-the-infamous-economic-meltdown/

"I found inspiration from Alfred Lansing's": Endurance: Shackleton's Incredible Voyage: Lansing, A. (1959). *Endurance: Shackleton's incredible voyage.* McGraw-Hill.

How To: Ask Better Questions: 3X5 Leadership. (n.d.). *How to ask better questions.* Retrieved 2024 from https://www.3x5leadership.com/blog/ask-better-questions;
Carney, D. (2023, November 3). *The science of having a great conversation. Wired.* Retrieved 2024 from

https://www.wired.com/story/the-science-of-having-a-great-conversation-research-social-connection;
Sutherland, S. (2021, June 15). *Build better processes by questioning everything. UX Design.* Retrieved 2024 from https://uxdesign.cc/build-better-processes-by-questioning-everything-81a8bfb7f21a

Stage Seven: Renewal

"President Obama famously spoke about the audacity of hope": Obama, B. (2004, July 27). *Keynote address at the Democratic National Convention.* Retrieved from https://www.c-span.org/video/?185437-1/keynote-address-barack-obama; Obama, B. (2006). *The audacity of hope: Thoughts on reclaiming the American dream.* Crown Publishers.

"Turtles, particularly the honu (green sea turtle), hold deep spiritual and cultural": U.S. Fish and Wildlife Service. (2023, August 4). *Species spotlight: Hawaiian green sea turtle (HONU).* U.S. Fish and Wildlife Service. https://www.fws.gov/story/species-spotlight-hawaiian-green-sea-turtle-honu; Maui Ocean Center. (2023, June 26). *Green sea turtles | Hawaiian marine life.* Maui Ocean Center. https://mauioceancenter.com/marine-life/hawaiian-green-sea-turtle

"In 1985, Steve Jobs was ousted from Apple": Directors Institute. (n.d.). *Why Steve Jobs was fired by Apple.* Directors Institute. Retrieved from https://www.directors-institute.com/post/whystevejobswasfiredbyapple; Biography.com Editors. (2020, April 16). *Steve Jobs: Pixar animation history.* Biography. Retrieved from https://www.biography.com/business-leaders/steve-jobs-pixar-animation-history;

McCaskill, A. (2013, July 9). *Today in Apple history: Steve Jobs leaves and rejoins Apple*. Cult of Mac. Retrieved from https://www.cultofmac.com/news/today-in-apple-history-steve-jobs-leaves-and-rejoins-apple

The Role of Intentions in Career Development: Jennings, T. E. (1996). *The role of intentions and task performance in career development* (Master's thesis, Loyola University Chicago). Loyola University Chicago eCommons. https://ecommons.luc.edu/luc_theses/4195

"The idea of finding your 'why' is not unlike Simon Sinek's concept": Sinek, S. (2009). *Start with why: How great leaders inspire everyone to take action.* Portfolio.

"While Apple has a legacy of rebelling against conformity": Apple Inc. (1984, January 22). *1984 Super Bowl commercial* [Video]. YouTube. https://www.youtube.com/watch?v=2zfqw8nhUwA

"He encouraged employees and consumers to 'Think Different' about technology": Gorman, M. (2017). *The "Think Different" campaign: How it helped rebrand Apple.* AdAge. https://adage.com/article/brand-marketing/think-different-campaign-helped-rebrand-apple/310865

About the Author

Born and raised in sunny San Diego, Steve Jaffe began his writing journey at San Diego State University, where he earned a bachelor's degree in journalism and communication. After a 25-year career in advertising and marketing—including work on the iconic "What Happens in Vegas Stays in Vegas" advertising campaign—he has returned to his writing roots. Throughout his career, Steve has built a reputation for creativity, strategic insight, and a deep understanding of human experiences.

Steve resides in Altadena, California, with his wife, two children, and a perpetually shedding dog. When he's not writing or consulting as a marketing expert, you can find him chasing waves along the coast or carving fresh powder on the slopes—always seeking balance and adventure in his professional and personal life. Steve's journey continues to be a testament to resilience, innovation, and the belief that sharing authentic experiences can inspire growth and lead to a deeper understanding of who we truly are.

www.ingramcontent.com/pod-product-compliance
Lightning Source LLC
Chambersburg PA
CBHW060834120626
46557CB00001B/494